Picasso as a Book Artist

A.   Frontispiece for Artaud's, *Autre chose que de l'enfant beau*, 1957.
Etching.

Picasso as a Book Artist

by

ABRAHAM HORODISCH

THE WORLD PUBLISHING COMPANY

CLEVELAND AND NEW YORK

Published by The World Publishing Company
2231 West 110th Street, Cleveland 2, Ohio

Library of Congress Catalog Card Number: 62–9048

FIRST EDITION

First published in 1957 under the title
Pablo Picasso als Buchkünstler
by Gesellschaft der Bibliophilen, Frankfurt am Main
This edition has been revised and expanded by the author

TRANSLATION BY
I. GRAFE

Contents

5

Illustrations

COLOUR PLATES

MONOCHROMES

Illustrations

Illustrations

Preface

Picasso's art as illustrator is representative of our time, and whatever later generations may think of present-day book decoration, they will not do it justice unless they take account of Picasso's work. But for all their importance, the books illustrated by this artist are very little known. The only extensive, if not quite complete, collection in Europe is that of the Bibliothèque Nationale in Paris, and another large collection, also incomplete, is owned by the Museum of Modern Art in New York. Elsewhere it is almost impossible to survey the whole oeuvre, and as some of the books were printed in very small editions and hardly ever appear on the market, and nearly all the others are also very valuable, few collectors will be in a position to acquire even the most important items.

These facts seemed a sufficient justification for undertaking the present study, which is, as far as we are aware, the first attempt at a detailed description and analysis of Picasso's work as illustrator.

We had the choice between different methods of approaching the subject. One was to consult the persons concerned, above all the artist himself, as well as authors and publishers (most of whom are still alive), and in this way to assemble as many facts as possible; another was to dispense with all personal enquiries and to let the books speak for themselves; yet a third was to combine the first two methods. After careful consideration we decided upon the second method because we were afraid of being led astray by personal information. Many of the books were published so long ago that memories were almost bound to be unreliable and even in the case of more recent works there was a danger that too subjective an interpretation of the facts, especially on the part of those directly concerned, might mislead the conscientious student. We thought it safer to base our researches upon the books alone. To arrive in a few instances

11

at erroneous conclusions seemed less harmful than to give currency to legends which can create greater confusion in the long run for being invested with an air of authority which later ages must take upon trust.

It is a pleasant duty to thank all those who have assisted us during the preparation of this study. First and foremost the Bibliothèque Nationale in Paris, and in particular M. Guignard, who is in charge of the Department of Rare Books ('Réserve'), and the members of his staff, who spared no trouble in placing their treasures at our disposal over and over again, and who allowed us also to consult their card index of illustrators, without which we could not have compiled our bibliography. Mme. Lacourière, the wife of the famous Paris copper engraver who printed many of Picasso's etchings on his hand-press, permitted us to inspect certain prints not to be found in the Bibliothèque Nationale, and she also gave us certain information about printing processes. We are equally grateful to the Municipal Museum in Amsterdam, whose excellent director, Jhr. W. J. H. B. Sandberg, showed himself extraordinarily generous: he specially purchased, at our suggestion, one of the rarest Picasso books, which was not to be found in any public library in Europe, and gave us the opportunity of examining and photographing it. Mr. Kloet, the librarian of this museum, was most helpful in giving us access to the books under his care before the library was opened to the public. We also wish to thank Colonel Daniel Sickles and M. Paul Bonet, both in Paris, and to Mr. A. J. Guépin in Eindhoven for their kindness in giving us permission to examine and describe books in their collections, as well as Dr. Bernhard Geiser, Berne, for readily answering our enquiries.

I am particularly grateful to M. Jean Hugues and M. Tristan Tzara in Paris and to M. P. A. Benoit in Alès for giving me information on many points, for drawing my attention to a number of bibliographical details and for allowing me to inspect and to photograph books in their possession. I owe a particular debt of gratitude to M. Benoit, through whose generosity I obtained access to some exceedingly rare publications, which I should hardly have been able to see without his assistance.

Introduction

A study dealing with Picasso as illustrator calls for a few introductory remarks on the principles underlying the illustrated book in general. We shall therefore turn very briefly to the origins of book illustration, approaching them without any preconceived ideas, in the same way that the modern movement in art, which numbers Picasso among its most eminent exponents, tries to grapple with all problems of artistic creation.

In our civilization the book conveys information, but it has not been used for this purpose at all times and everywhere. Originally it may have served as an instrument of magic, just as prehistoric cave-paintings are interpreted as magical incantations and just as Ethiopian magical scrolls with their texts and illustrations were used until recently — and indeed are perhaps still being used — not to convey information or as a means of edification, but for purely occult purposes. In the Western world such works are an insignificant exception. Even in the occult books of medieval and later sorcerers the illustrations are generally intended to clarify the instructions given to the adept.

Illustrated books in the form familiar to us are the descendants of medieval illuminated codices. In some of these, pictures were added to elucidate the text where author or scribe regarded the words alone as insufficient, others were decorated for purposes of ostentation. We must have no illusions as to their origin: the patrons who commissioned these codices were not usually prompted by a deep love of art, but in most instances by no more than a wish to add to their prestige with friend and foe by the possession of something valuable and extraordinary. For this purpose an illustrated manuscript was particularly suitable, since most of those whom the owner wished to impress were illiterate and susceptible only to pictures: the more sumptuous the gilding, the greater was the effect. Those patrons who could not afford extensive illumination contented

13

1.   Illustration to a story by Pio Baroja in the periodical *Arte Joven,*
1901. *See page 18*

themselves with rubricated chapter-headings, with more or less elaborately decorated initials and — when their means allowed — with decorated borders or a pictorial representation on the first page.

If many patrons cared little for the manuscript itself, many illuminators showed equally little regard for their texts. A few artists, it is true, showed full understanding of what such a task demanded and fitted their work to a given text; many more, however, kept within the established traditions, repeating the same Saints with the same customary attributes; after all, they could hardly go far wrong, since the same prayers recurred in their Missals and Books of Hours. Whether the texts are of a legal, literary or liturgical character, we find the same decorated borders with the same beasts and plants. Any bookseller who can offer a manuscript containing a less hackneyed illumination will lay great stress on the fact in his catalogue.

After the invention of printing, the nature of the illustrated book underwent a change. The book itself enjoyed wider circulation and, whereas previously it had reached but a few, it now became more and more a tool of scholars and clerics. Their interest, however, was limited to the texts; illustrations were confined to popular books and served to amuse the masses, who were still illiterate. In 1492, about forty years after the invention of movable type, there appeared the first illustrated 'de luxe' edition, the famous *Nuremberg Chronicle*, which was expressly intended to be a *de luxe* book, as is shown in the extant correspondence of the publisher, Koberger. But his letters also tell us that this novelty did not prove as successful with the public as he had expected. More than another generation was to pass, until, as a result of the emblem books brought into fashion by Alciati and of the perfection of the woodcut through Dürer, Holbein and others, illustrated suites, accompanied by more or less text, and illustrated editions of literary works gained favour in book-buying circles. This trend came to an end about the beginning of the seventeenth century and from then on great care and considerable expense were lavished on documentary illustrations engraved in copper, especially for books on topography, geography and science.

We need not dwell upon the development of documentary illustration, which is nowadays generally based upon photography, to the exclusion of the creative artist, so as to eliminate all subjective interpretation. The few remaining exceptions merely prove the rule and can here be left out of account as Picasso was never active in this field.[1]

Towards the end of the seventeenth century, suites of copper engravings and books illustrated with such engravings began to attract a much wider circle of buyers in Holland (Jan Luyken and Romijn de Hooghe) and in Germany (Nuremberg and Augsburg prints), and the French Rococo was the golden age of illustrated *éditions de luxe*, i.e. works of literature beautifully printed and preciously decorated with illustrations.

Since then books of this kind have continued to enjoy popularity in most European countries. Technical advances such as colour gravure printing, Bewick's revival of wood engraving and the invention of lithography have opened up unexpected possibilities, which have been exploited to the full during the past hundred and fifty years. By the beginning of the present century book design in Western Europe had surpassed that of earlier times in so far as production methods were concerned. Though the average quality of paper has gone down, a small number of mills still produce paper of the highest traditional qualities, and fine Chinese and Japanese papers are being regularly imported. The revival of fine book production, initiated in England by William Morris and T. J. Cobden-Sanderson, began to raise the low level of typography throughout Western Europe and before long some printers in every country were able to point to achievements that were in no way inferior to those of earlier centuries. The Romantic movement had brought about a relaxation of the old rigid rules of book architecture and, though occasional lapses and eccentricities were not avoided, there was now scope for an amusing and lively play of forms such as had hitherto been unknown.

In one point only there had been no change for four hundred years: the illustrator was still expected to follow the text closely. Any deviation was out of the question and even the most revolutionary Impressionist artists, Toulouse-Lautrec, Bonnard and Slevogt, would not have dreamt of straying from the literary conceptions of the poet.

That was the situation in the first decade of the present century, when the younger generation entered upon the heritage of their fathers and tried to fill the old skins with new wine.

The space at our disposal does not permit a detailed description of the artistic movements that arose in those years. We must assume the reader to be familiar with them and we cannot even attempt to analyse Picasso's art and its development, although his art as illustrator is only a part of, and only fully intelligible within the context of, his oeuvre as a whole. We can do no more than give a few brief indications whenever they seem necessary and refer the reader to more general works (the literature on Picasso alone fills many shelves).[2] Even within the narrower compass of our study we shall encounter a host of problems.

That the young Picasso was but little active as illustrator is hardly an accident. Artists who grapple so intensively with problems of form need, it would seem, a direct approach to the actual phenomena by which they are surrounded and have no use for the intermediary of another art such as literature. Great artists who are also great illustrators are found at the end of a period of development

ES-SERVEIX-BEURE-Y-MENJAR-A-TOTES-HORES

PERE ROMEU – 4 GATS

CARRER D MONTESIÓN·

2. Advertisement for Picasso's favourite restaurant in Barcelona, 'Els quatre gats', 1897. (After Alexandre Cirici-Pellicer.) *See page 19*

rather than at the beginning. The art of the woodcut had been practised for more than a hundred years before it reached perfection in Dürer and Holbein; after them came still many other great masters, but the woodcut as art form went into decline and finally broke down at the end of the sixteenth century. On the other hand it might have been expected that Rembrandt, a master of the graphic arts resident in Amsterdam, the printing and publishing centre of Northern Europe in the seventeenth century, would be flooded with publishers' commissions; the fact is that he worked as an illustrator only very occasionally, and his numerous etchings of Biblical subjects are clearly free graphic inventions, not illustrations. Any so-called 'Rembrandt Bible' betrays at once the calculating publisher, who had to do violence to the artist's work as well as to Holy Scripture in order to compile a 'handsome book'.

Picasso as a Book Artist

Picasso's art evolved not in the solitude of a studio remote from the world, but at the centre of the contemporary art world, where he was in constant touch and exchanged ideas with like-minded friends. It is significant that his early encounters with books were chance encounters brought about not by his relation to literature but by his relations with people. Equally illuminating is a conversation which the present writer had, while he was preparing the text of this study, with a personal friend of Picasso's, who is also thoroughly familiar with the artist's oeuvre. This connoisseur put forward the view, which greatly astonished the writer and which, had it been justified, would have deprived this study of its theme, that Picasso had never been an illustrator and had not illustrated a single book in his whole life; some publishers had indeed made up books by combining their own texts with prints by the artist — but that was all. When the writer's objections showed this view to be hardly tenable, the other, undoubtedly a serious and knowledgeable man, conceded that Picasso had occasionally read certain manuscripts and, inspired by them, had created free graphic designs, which had subsequently been printed with those texts, but illustrations, it was repeated, he had never made.

These pronouncements are, as we shall see, partly at variance with the facts and partly over-subtle formulations of an original mind. We shall nevertheless do well to bear them in mind in order to recall them wherever they are valid and, where necessary, to treat our own conclusions with reserve.

Fernande Olivier, for many years Picasso's companion, has stated that Picasso does not read a great deal[3] and Jaime Sabartés, a friend of his early years and later his secretary, goes so far as to say he cannot remember seeing Picasso with a book in his hand; he adds, however, that in conversation he had found Picasso to be well acquainted with works of literature[4] (elsewhere in his book, Sabartés suggests that the artist may have read much in bed at night). As a young man Picasso had literary inclinations, as is shown by his connection in 1901 with a short-lived Spanish review, *Arte Joven*.[5] This periodical, which ran to five issues in all, published Picasso's earliest drawings and also announced a book on Madrid with drawings by him and text by Francisco de A. Soler. This book was never published, but four illustrations for it appeared in *Arte Joven*, as did also an illustration to a story by Pio Baroja (fig. 1), a recognizably youthful work, which in no way foreshadows the artist's later development.[6]

18

3.   Ex-libris for Camilo Bargiela, 1901. *See pages 19–20*

A few other works of the same period are worth mentioning in this context. A drawing for an advertisement of 'Els quatre gats' (The Four Cats) in Barcelona, a favourite haunt of the artist and his circle (fig. 2), dates from 1897. These portraits of himself and his friends[7] may be of importance for the Picasso biographer; the execution is not distinguished by particular originality and we register the drawing simply as one of Picasso's few excursions into applied graphic art. His lack of interest in this field is confirmed by the *ex-libris* for

4. Letter from Picasso to Reventós. Paris, 1900.
(After Cirici-Pellicer.) *See page 21*

Introduction

Camilo Bargiela (fig. 3), a free drawing in which a portrait caricature takes the place of the owner's name. It is of considerable interest for the artist's youthful style, but the superimposed words EX-LIBRIS make it in no way a true book-plate: one can see that Picasso had not taken the trouble to study the special requirements of an *ex-libris*. Of greater interest for our purpose is an illustrated letter of November 19, 1900, to his friend Ramon Reventós (fig. 4): writing and drawing are here distributed with a sure feeling for balance, and we shall see that a page such as this can be regarded as the harbinger of works created many decades later.

The very first book containing an original graphic work by Picasso is one from which no conclusions can be drawn. When André Salmon, then an unknown young man, though he has since won for himself a place in French literature, published a small volume of poems in 1905, Picasso, with whom he was on friendly terms, contributed an etching for the *édition de luxe* (about ten copies on Japanese paper — the exact number can no longer be ascertained). It is reproduced here (fig. 5) because it was the artist's earliest print to appear in a book as well as on account of its great rarity: a man and a boy in bathing costumes — a typical early work and without special importance in the artist's oeuvre. We have read Salmon's poems — which Picasso may or may not have done — and have found only one (on page 85) with which the etching may perhaps be connected:

POUR L'AMI PIERROT

Quand cette nuit finira-t-elle?
Je sais qu'au loin quelqu'un m'appelle.
Pierrot,
Mon ami Pierrot,
As-tu rallumé ta chandelle?

Quel mal secret me paralyse?
Seul et nu mon frère agonise;
Pierrot,
Mon ami Pierrot,
Pierrot, prête-moi ta chandelle.

Je sais maintenant qui m'appelle,
Aux mille cierges de la chapelle.
Pierrot,
Mon ami Pierrot,
Va donc rallumer ta chandelle. . . .

Even if the etching should have been inspired by this poem — and it must be doubted — it does not strike the same morbid, elegiac note.[8]

The case is quite different with the first literary work for which Picasso made illustrations in the true sense: the two parts of *Saint Matorel* by Max Jacob. Once again personal circumstances played a decisive part. Jacob had been so much impressed by Picasso's first exhibition (at Vollard's in 1901) that he went to see the artist, on the pretext that he wished to write a book about him. This book was never written (the first monograph on Picasso was not to appear until twenty years later and its author was Raynal), but the meeting led to a long friendship, which bore fruit in the illustrations that Picasso made ten and twelve years later.

The first volume, entitled *Saint Matorel*, depicts the life of a Parisian *petit bourgeois*, who leads a humdrum existence like millions of others, but is not proof against simple everyday temptations and steals from a friend. He then begins to realize the vanity of his life, converts first himself and then his friend, enters a monastery and dies a deeply pious man. He goes to Heaven, where he again encounters various temptations, but from these trials he emerges victorious and is finally canonized.

While the first volume is for the greatest part a prose narrative, the second, entitled *Le Siège de Jérusalem; grande tentation céleste de Saint Matorel,* is in the form of a drama in three acts. Jacob has explained its symbolism in the following words: 'La Jérusalem de Saint Jean n'est que le symbole de la perfection divine, sa description symbolise les vertus constitutives de cette perfection.' Several princes with their armies fight for the key to this heavenly Jerusalem, but Saint Matorel, at the cost of his life, throws the key into the water, where it is lost for ever, and all who have striven for the heavenly Jerusalem perish in the struggle.

Picasso's four etchings to *Saint Matorel* date from 1910, the beginning of the

5.   Frontispiece to the *édition de luxe* of André Salmon, *Poèmes*, 1905.
Geiser, *Picasso peintre-graveur*, No. 6. *See page 21*

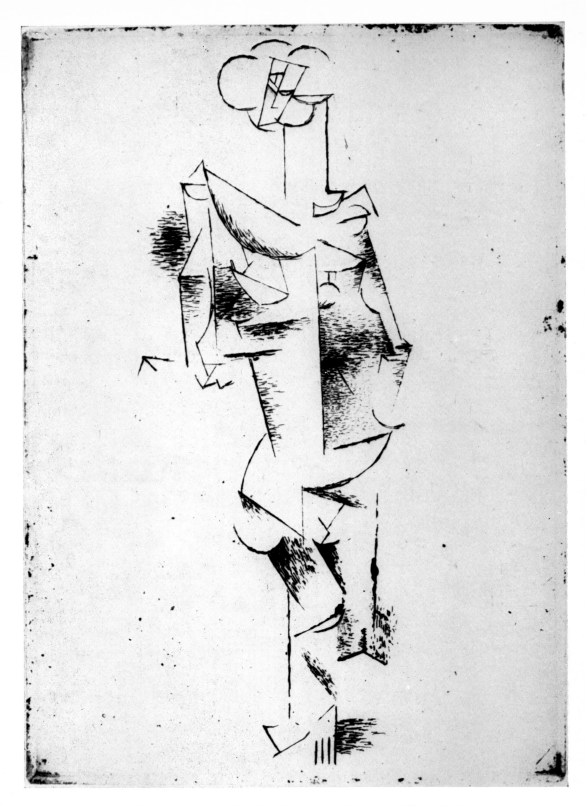

6.   Illustration to Max Jacob, *Saint Matorel*, 1911. Etching,
original size. Geiser, ib. No. 23. *See page 23*

7.   Illustration to Max Jacob, *Saint Matorel*, 1911. Etching,
original size. Geiser, ib. No. 24. *See page 23*

8.   Illustration to Max Jacob, *Le Siège de Jérusalem*, 1914. Etching,
original size. Geiser, ib. No. 35. *See page 23*

analytical-cubist period. They represent: Mademoiselle Léonie (a commonplace middle-class girl — Part One, second chapter; fig. 6); the table (at a village inn where Matorel as commercial traveller meets company — Part One, fifth chapter; fig. 7); Mademoiselle Léonie, this time on a chaiselongue; and finally the monastery of the Lazarists in Barcelona,[9] the scene of the decisive debate between Matorel and his converted friend. Just as the text is to be understood symbolically, so Picasso's prints strike us not as representing individual persons or situations, but as formulas expressing the essence of the subject. We are not here concerned with what the artist was trying to achieve in these prints, but with the beholder's reaction to them. He will hardly see in this Mademoiselle Léonie the portrait of an individual girl, or in the table a particular object in a particular room. The monastery (not here reproduced) is not a particular building — though Picasso may have had one in mind — but simply a monastery. And in the same way as we must lift the poet's characters above the individual plane in order to understand them aright, so the illustrations, in conformity with the text, strike the beholder as symbolic ciphers rather than as visual representations.

The illustrations to *Le Siège de Jérusalem* are much harder to interpret. They date from the artist's synthetic-cubist period, about 1913, and differ strikingly in formal conception from those to *Saint Matorel*. The artist has entitled the three etchings: Female Nude (fig. 8), Still-Life with Skull,[10] and Woman.[10a] The first print could be linked, if tenuously, with the 'jeune sauvage' who together with the 'vieille sauvage', personifies that part of mankind which keeps aloof from the fight for the heavenly Jerusalem, but the other two must be regarded, it seems, as decorative additions of small relevance to Jacob's text. Oddly enough, if we were unaware of the titles Picasso has given them, we should feel tempted to interpret both prints as somehow related to the story. We might have imagined that the second chapter, which takes place in the camp of the princes laying siege to Jerusalem, was illustrated with a vision of the disputed city, for the 'Still-Life with Skull' is reminiscent of a dream fortress with embattled towers; and that the third Act, of which the second scene takes place in the assembly hall, had inspired a construction not unlike the interior of a room.

These two volumes, published in 1911 and 1914, must be considered landmarks in the history of modern book illustration. They constitute the earliest

MAX JACOB

SAINT MATOREL

Illustré d'eaux-fortes

par

PABLO PICASSO

PARIS

HENRY KAHNWEILER, EDITEUR

28 Rue Vignon 28

9.   Title page of Max Jacob, *Saint Matorel*, 1911. *See page 25*

attempt to break with tradition, though in *Saint Matorel* the artist's conception had not yet undergone a complete change. He still intended, in the usual way, to create visual representations of persons and objects appearing in the text, but the use of cubist constructions forced him to forgo realistic forms. Thus he had to create prints which, instead of actually illustrating the text, are visual equivalents inspired by the artistic tenor of the words: not graphic representations of single episodes, but interpretations of the book's spirit. This approach is comparable in principle to that of medieval illuminators, who instead of illustrating the prayers in a Book of Hours, represented a certain Saint with his attributes, or Christ in Glory, merely because Christ or the Saint was named in a prayer. Although the result is not an illustration of the text in the strict sense, we feel that word and image have been brought into perfect harmony. Nowadays the manner in which the *Matorel* volumes are illustrated no longer causes surprise: Picasso himself as well as others have made it familiar enough. But in 1911 and 1914 these were novel and unheard-of experiments, which perplexed the connoisseurs, were ridiculed by bibliophiles, and taken seriously by very few. No wonder that the publisher produced no more than a hundred copies of both volumes — and one wonders how long it took him to sell this number.

The drawing for the publisher's device on the title-page of *Saint Matorel* was made by Derain (fig. 9). Kahnweiler probably believed that Picasso was not at his best in the field of applied graphic art. But later on, as we shall see, the artist was to produce some successful designs of great charm for practical use.

In 1918, during the first World War, appeared *Le Coq et l'arlequin* by Jean Cocteau. The artistic tendency of the book finds expression in the following passage, which the author placed at the head of his text: 'J'admire les Arlequins de Cézanne et de Picasso mais je n'aime pas l'Arlequin. Il porte un loup et un costume de *toutes les couleurs*. Après avoir renié au chant du coq, il se cache. C'est un coq de la nuit. — Par contre j'aime le vrai coq, *profondément bariolé*. Le coq dit Cocteau deux fois et habite sa ferme . . . Arlequin signifie encore: mets composés de restes divers (Larousse).' The cock symbolizes idealism and purity of intention, harlequin personifies the opportunist time-server. Picasso contributed two drawings, which have no special importance within his oeuvre as a whole; but they are so attractive and, in their almost calligraphic quality, so well suited to the printed page that we reproduce both of them (fig. 10).

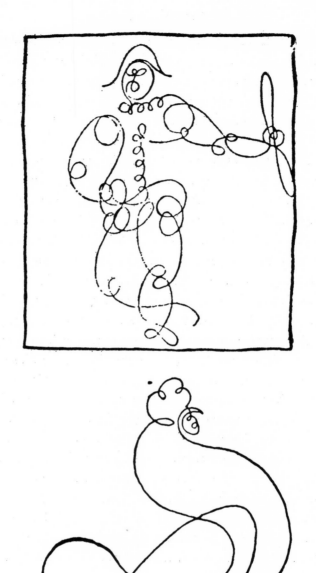

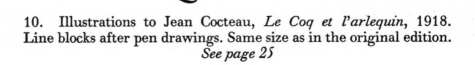

10.   Illustrations to Jean Cocteau, *Le Coq et l'arlequin*, 1918.
Line blocks after pen drawings. Same size as in the original edition.
See page 25

Introduction

Of much greater importance is the next book with illustrations by Picasso: *Le Manuscrit trouvé dans un chapeau* by André Salmon, with thirty-eight drawings printed from line blocks. This book appears to justify the thesis propounded by the artist's friend quoted above, for it was published in 1919 while the illustrations reproduce drawings made many years before. The text is made up of short sketches, nearly all of them in prose, except for three in poetic form and two others with verses interspersed. The drawings, which were completed long before the text was even begun, harmonize with it to perfection, and as most of them are of outstanding artistic quality the volume as a whole is very attractive even though its genesis runs counter to all principles of sound book design.

How was that possible? First it must be pointed out that the book designer — Salmon himself — acquitted himself with admirable ingenuity. It seems likely that he did not decide upon the lay-out of the illustrations until after the type had been set up. This procedure allowed him to be guided by aesthetic considerations in determining their sizes: some of the drawings fill the pages, while others, in reduced size, either fit perfectly into the type or form charming tail-vignettes. Salmon's skill may be judged from the example reproduced here (fig. 11). This drawing shows the preliminaries to a duel between two grotesque nude figures, in the background are four equally grotesque seconds or witnesses, whose nakedness is emphasized with particular scurrility by their only covering, a solemn top hat. What led Picasso to make this drawing we do not know. Salmon places it at the head of a sketch, entitled 'Reveillon', which describes, with grotesque and sarcastic humour, a banquet attended by famous personalities of the past — Chopin, Ninon de Lenclos, Gilles de Rais, Gautier and others. The comic unreality of this fantasy is matched by the comic unreality of the nudes and it is not felt as incongruous that the words make no mention of a duel, while the drawing offers no possible parallel to the contents of the sketch. Elsewhere however, the poet has contrived so close a correspondence between word and drawing that one cannot help suspecting that he wrote a sketch, or even altered a passage in proof, to suit a particular Picasso drawing. We do not refer in the first place to the sketch 'Une femme nue', which has two female nudes on the opposite page:[11] there are so many nudes among Picasso's drawings that the choice must have been easy enough. But we also find a dance scene set into the poem 'Danseuse aux perles', and if in a poem entitled 'Ombres', in which Salmon

27

11.   Illustration from André Salmon, *Le manuscrit trouvé dans un chapeau*, 1919. Line-block after a pen drawing. 100 × 163 mm.
See page 27

conjures up the shades of Parisian writers of the past, the words 'Et cette allée du Luxembourg, où chaque soir je puis saluer ton ombre, Moréas. . . .' are promptly followed by a portrait of Jean Moréas with his autograph signature, then it is hard to regard this as a pure coincidence. The same applies to the inspired arabesque of an elderly man with bent back, bald but for a thin ring of curly hair, which is used as tail-piece on a page entitled 'Epigramme' and containing a sentence that, though witty enough, seems more suitable for a comic paper than for a work of literary pretensions: 'Il y avait une fois un poète si pauvre, si mal logé et si dépourvu que, lorsque l'Académie Française lui offrit un fauteuil, il demanda la permission de l'emporter chez soi.'

Introduction

To three books published before Salmon's *Manuscrit trouvé dans un chapeau* Picasso had contributed a print for the *édition de luxe*. The two etchings in *Le Cornet à dés* and *Le Phanérogame* by Max Jacob (1917) have no connection with the texts, and Guillaume Apollinaire's fine *Calligrammes* (1918) has a portrait of the poet engraved in wood by R. Jandon after a drawing by Picasso; the first four copies of the edition contain a second portrait of Apollinaire by Picasso, etched by Jandon. Picasso and Apollinaire were close friends and for some years used to meet every day. The artist made numerous portraits of the poet and for many years after the latter's premature death such portrait drawings by Picasso continued to be published. These have no claim to be regarded as illustrations and the same applies in the case of another sixty-seven books published between 1908 and 1959, to which the artist contributed a portrait of the author or some other graphic work, whether a drawing or an original print.

The drawing which Picasso made in 1919 for the cover of Stravinsky's *Ragtime* (fig. 12) is a true book decoration. It is an inspired, one might almost say calligraphic, pen sketch of two musicians, for which Picasso seems to have drawn upon recollections of his frequent visits to the Circus Medrano in earlier years. But the necessary text (the indispensable minimum: composer, title and publisher) is arranged in an almost childish way: a frame of three lines and between them, quite haphazard, the few words written hastily in clumsy capital letters, slightly off-centre. Not until many years later did Picasso realize that his natural handwriting offered much greater aesthetic possibilities than such awkward capitals.

Three years later, in 1922, appeared a slender volume of poems by Pierre Reverdy, *Cravates de Chanvre*, in an edition limited to 125 copies. The *édition de luxe* (Nos. 1–15 on Japanese paper and Nos. 16–30 on deckle-edged paper) contains three etchings by Picasso, the other copies only one, a frontispiece showing the poet seated on a chair and reading. The two prints in the text bear no relation to the poems, expressionist renderings of moods inspired by city and countryside, with such titles as 'Le flot berceur', 'Le Littoral', 'Cheminée d'usine', 'Temps couvert', and so on. One of the two etchings represents three women in Grecian costumes at a fountain, the other a number of bathing women: a group of four on the beach, another nearby sunbathing, another seated by the water, two splashing in the water, and a ninth about to dive from a high board.

12. Wrapper of Igor Stravinsky, *Ragtime*, 1919. Line-block after a
pen drawing. 279 × 227 mm. *See page 29*

But it would be mistaken to expect a connection between this print and the poem entitled 'Le Littoral'. This reads:

> *La teinte grise au cadran lumineux*
> > *Au cadran sans aiguïlles*
> > *Au regard bleu*
> *Au bord de cette ville*
> > *Dont le clocher s'endort*
> *Près du bois et des plis*
> > *Le vent et ses efforts*
> *Comme le boulevard roule sur les murailles*
> > *Et les arbres qui rôdent dans la nuit*
> *Les formes du silence*
> > *Et de l'eau*
> > *Dans le bruit*
> *Les franges de la mer*
> *Les cœurs en engrenage*
> *Et tout le mouvement conquis*
> > *Sur le passage*
> *La lumière découpe des sillons*
> *Une rue se détache*
> > *Un couloir*
> > *Des maisons*
> *L'œil veille sur les toits*
> > *Le regard coule au fond*
> *Mais le ciel s'arrondit plus bas à l'horizon.*

In style as well as in mood the prints are quite unrelated to the words, for their classicistic realism does not match the expressionism of the poetry. We have here a clear case of the arbitrary combination of a text with prints which Picasso presented to the poet as a token of their friendship.

It is not until the end of 1931 that we find another book with numerous illustrations by Picasso: Balzac's *Le Chef-d'œuvre inconnu*. The number of illustrations is indeed considerable: the sixteen introductory pages have 56 drawings, the text, including title-page and verso, has another 67, and in addition there are 13 full-page etchings.

The publisher was Ambroise Vollard, the famous Paris art-dealer, who, as a hobby rather than as a business venture, brought out a number of books. These fetch high prices in France and abroad, and some of them are among the best-designed books of our time.

Vollard's publications have been listed in a bibliography[12] and his memoirs contain several references to his publishing activities. This is not the place to analyse the part he played in this field. His admirers have nothing but praise for all his publications, while many other bibliophiles were too narrow-minded and biased to allow him any merit whatever. Perhaps it is fair to sum up Vollard's publishing achievements roughly as follows: an illustrated book was, for him, in the first place a book with original prints from the hand of a great artist, while he considered the relation of the illustrations to the text, and to the overall design, of secondary importance. At the same time he had as fine an appreciation of the quality of paper and printing as of artistic achievement. The result was that all his books are beautifully printed and most are illustrated by great artists, but the books as such are not always of the same standard. The greatest of the artists who collaborated with him were Bonnard, Degas, Maillol, Picasso, Rodin and Rouault, and the classic example of a book in which he was eminently successful is the famous edition of Longus's *Daphnis and Chloe* with the lithographs of Bonnard (1912).

These few words about Vollard seemed necessary because *Le Chef-d'œuvre inconnu* is his work to the same extent as *Le Manuscrit trouvé dans un chapeau* is that of Salmon. The publication of Balzac's book with illustrations by Picasso was his idea and it is easy to see how he came to think of it. The scene of the well-known story is laid in Paris in the year 1622. Poussin, then a shy young art student who had just arrived from his home in Picardie, visits the famous painter Pourbus in his studio. There he meets an eccentric old man named Frenhofer, who proves to be an eminent master of the art of painting and who tells wonders of the only perfect picture of his time, a woman's portrait painted by himself, the only pupil of the great Mabuse. He had been working on it for ten years and had guarded its secret jealously, but Pourbus and Poussin persuade him to show them the picture. When they stand before it they discover that innumerable overpaintings have turned it into a confusion of meaningless smudges and that the perfection of which Frenhofer had spoken is but the delusion of a half-crazed genius.

The problem concealed behind this fable, the tension between the beholder's objective perception on the one hand and the artist's intention and formal structure on the other, springs into full relief when we remember how the critics and the public reacted to the cubism of the youthful Picasso. Moreover many of Balzac's remarks in this story may have echoed Picasso's own thoughts.[13] Thus it is easy to see why he warmed to Vollard's project and promised to contribute the illustrations.

Let us now examine in detail this book, which arouses the enthusiasm of so many lovers of modern art and which Barr[14] calls one of the most remarkable illustrated books of our time. It starts with a kind of introduction by Picasso (described as such by Vollard in the book), the sixteen pages already mentioned, containing fifty-six strange drawings made up entirely of systems of straight and curved lines with circular dots at their ends and intersections. These drawings come from a sketch-book of 1926 and are characterized by Barr as follows: ' . . . drawings unlike any he had made before. . . . A few vaguely suggest . . . musical instruments, others seem abstract. . . . All seem done absentmindedly or automatically as if they were doodles.' As Picasso has always denied that he ever created 'abstract' works, most of these strange patterns are probably to be interpreted as attempts to reduce musical instruments to an unusual formula not readily understood by the beholder (fig. 13). Even Gieure,[15] who neglects hardly any aspect of Picasso's work and analyses all phases of his artistic career, has nothing to say about these drawings, although he expressly mentions the Balzac;[16] instead he praises the realistic drawings, which we shall discuss presently and to which he refers — in our opinion mistakenly — as illustrations to *Le Chef-d'œuvre inconnu.*

Why Vollard has called the fifty-six drawings a kind of introduction (his heading reads: En manière d'introduction par Pablo Picasso) remains a mystery. The only explanation which has been advanced, that he intended to ridicule the artist by prefacing the text with this series of barely intelligible prints as a parallel to Frenhofer's supposed masterpiece,[17] is to be rejected outright. Nothing could have been farther from his mind, and he even intended to use

c

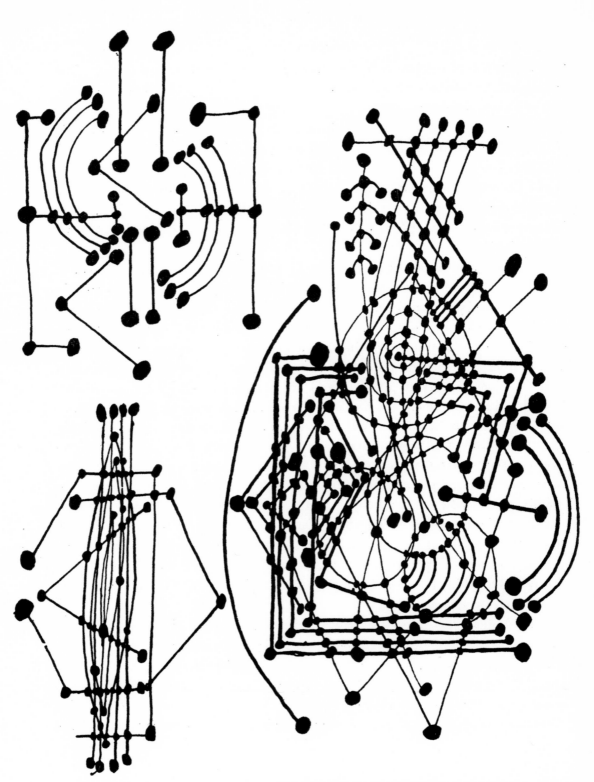

13.   One of the introductory series of drawings in Balzac, *Le Chef-d'oeuvre inconnu*, 1931. Pen drawing. 296 × 224 mm. *See page 33*

14.   Illustration from Balzac, *Le Chef-d'oeuvre inconnu*, 1931.
Wood engraving after a pen drawing. Original size. *See page 38*

15.   Half-page illustration from Balzac, *Le Chef-d'oeuvre inconnu,*
1931. Etching. Original size. *See page 38*

16. Full-page illustration from Balzac, *Le Chef-d'oeuvre inconnu*,
1931. Etching. 194 × 280 mm. Geiser, ib. No. 126. *See page 38*

the remaining drawings of the series in another book illustrated by Picasso (see below pp. 39–42). He took this 'introduction' quite seriously.

The sixty-seven drawings in the text, engraved in wood by Aubert, are for the greater part strongly stylized and in the cubist idiom (fig. 14). Some of Picasso's friends, who have seen the originals, declare that the wood engravings are only imperfect renderings. The subjects are varied: heads, nudes, still-lifes, a horse, etc., all quite unrelated to the text; Vollard had evidently made an arbitrary selection from the master's sketch-books and portfolios. Four of the illustrations (dated 1925 and 1926) are in a different, realistic style, and one of these, representing a man painting the portrait of a woman, can even to some extent be connected with the text (fig. 15).

Then follow the etchings. Though doubtless of the highest artistic quality, and probably responsible for the high esteem in which the book is held, most of them too have no connection whatever with the text. (Picasso made some more prints of this kind, e.g. the three reproduced in the periodical, *Minotaure*, I, 1, p. 24.) Among them are animal studies, studio scenes and other subjects, but only one that can possibly be regarded as an illustration to *Le Chef-d'œuvre inconnu*: an artist sketching a seated woman on a canvas, on which one sees nothing but a tangle of curves, some of them suggestive of geometry (fig. 16). Barr regards this print as coming nearest to illustrating Balzac's story. In our opinion the contrast between the realistic plasticity of the model and the abstract curves on the canvas does not warrant such a conclusion and was not even intended by Picasso. We believe that all he did was to represent the first sketch for the portrait, without any reference to the model or to Frenhofer's picture.

One curiosity must not remain unnoticed. At the end of the book Vollard has provided instructions to the bookbinder for the placing of the prints, but as the etchings were not numbered, the binder had no means of telling where each was to be placed. To remedy this, Picasso etched a thirteenth plate, divided into twelve numbered panels of approximately equal size, and indicated in each with a few lines the etching concerned. This unusual kind of register (we can recall only one parallel, in an illustrated French book of the Romantic period) has provided us with an extra print to which its sketchiness lends a special charm.[18]

If we now consider the book not in detail but as a whole, we can sum up as follows: the type is well set and printed on deckle-edged paper (the *édition de luxe* on Japanese paper); the first sixteen pages contain drawings which correspond neither with the contents nor with the form of the book and are extraneous to it; in the text there are drawings which lack all connection with it, which represent different stylistic periods (cubist and realistic), and which are said to be inadequate renderings of the originals; finally, a series of thirteen etchings, which for all their beauty have no more in common with Balzac's story. In a monograph dealing with an artist's development one expects as comprehehsive a treatment as possible of his successive styles; but an illustrated novel calls for a certain homogeneity, which meets the requirements of the text to some extent. This is here lacking altogether. To add to the confusion, Vollard prefaces the novel with an essay by Albert Besnard, which is quite amusing, but does less than justice to Balzac's story and would have been more appropriate in any other context than in a bibliophile edition. In our view, therefore, *Le Chef-d'œuvre inconnu* does not redound to the credit of Vollard, but must be regarded as one of his failures. That Picasso himself did not agree with Vollard's ideas will be seen from his next illustrated books, the *Métamorphoses* of Ovid and the *Lysistrata* of Aristophanes. But first a few words about a book which almost remained unpublished.

About the same time Vollard planned another book with illustrations by Picasso: André Suarès, *Hélène chez Archimède*. The illustrations are in existence — one etching and twenty-one drawings engraved on wood by Aubert. Nearly two decades were to pass until the text was first published, in 1949, as ordinary edition and without illustrations. A reading of the text gives little cause for regret that Vollard did not carry out this project. The book is a purely intellectual discussion, mostly in dialogue form, between the world of abstract reasoning, represented by Archimedes, and the world of physical existence, personified by Helen of Troy. Greek mythology, Mexican mythology and Indian philosophy are all brought into play, there is no action, only arguments similar to those in Plato's dialogues. In 1955 the book was published by the Nouveau Cercle Parisien du Livre with Picasso's old illustrations, and it is interesting to compare this edition with what we know of Vollard's plans.

The sumptuous folio (31·5 × 42·5 cm.) is set in a large size of an elegant Roman type and well printed on hand-made paper. Vollard had planned an 'introduction', similar to that in the Balzac, consisting of the remaining line

LIVRE PREMIER

JE me propose de dire les métamorphoses des corps en des corps nouveaux;
ô dieux, (car ces métamorphoses sont aussi votre ouvrage) secondez mon
entreprise de votre souffle et conduisez sans interruption ce poème depuis
les plus lointaines origines du monde jusqu'à mon temps.

17.   Half-page illustration to Ovide, *Les Métamorphoses*, 1931.
Etching. 145 × 170 mm. Geiser, ib. No. 143. *See page 43*

18.   Full-page illustration to Ovide, *Les Métamorphoses*, 1931.
Etching. 225 × 170 mm. Geiser, ib. No. 152. *See page 43*

drawings from the sketch-book of 1926. This has been omitted, but two of the drawings are used as normal illustrations in the text (pp. 77 and 165). The etching and one of the wood engravings have also been left out. It is not known how Vollard intended to use the three ornamental drawings, which now appear as full-page illustrations (pp. 47, 115 and 145). The volume contains altogether twenty-two drawings, of which two — male figures — are placed at the beginning and the end of the text as head- and tail-pieces, while the others appear as full-page illustrations and are printed on a paper which is different from that used for the text. We believe that Vollard would not have used two kinds on paper, since the wood engravings of the Balzac drawings are printed with the type. The illustrations have no connection with the text, except for the frontispiece, which shows a man in conversation with a woman.

The total result is very surprising. The fact that the drawings appear not in the text but on separate plates has softened the divergence between word and image. The effect is almost that of an independent accompaniment which is in the same key and in the same spirit as the text, and one is left with an impression of much greater homogeneity than one had been prepared to expect. But twenty-two long years had overlaid the text and the drawings with a kind of common patina.

The *Métamorphoses* of Ovid, an impressive quarto volume, came out towards the end of 1931. The text, a prose translation by Georges Lafaye, was printed by Léon Pichon, one of the best French printers. The classical calm of the type is broken by red initials, three lines deep, at the beginning of each section. Picasso made 30 etchings for this book, 15 full-page, the other 15 about half-page and used as head-pieces at the opening of each of the 15 Books. The full-page illustrations represent the following episodes: (1) Deucalion and Pyrrha creating a new human race; (2) Phaethon falling from the chariot of Phoebus; (3) the loves of Jupiter and Semele; (4) the daughters of Minyas refusing to acknowledge the god Bacchus; (5) Perseus and Phineus fighting for Andromeda; (6) Tereus assaulting his sister-in-law Philomela; (7) Cephalus accidentally killing his wife Procris; (8) Meleager slaying the boar of Calydon; (9) Hercules killing the Centaur Nessus; (10) Eurydice bitten by a snake; (11) the death of Orpheus; (12) Nestor telling of the war against Troy; (13) Polyxena, daughter of Priam, is sacrificed on the tomb of Achilles; (14) Vertumnus pursuing Pomona; (15) Numa as pupil of Pythagoras. We have here visual representations of scenes from the poem and consequently illustrations in the full sense of the word. The half-page etchings, on the other hand, differ in conception: here we find heads, or scenes from life, sometimes (e.g. in Book XIV) sketches of parts of the body.[19]

All the etchings are strictly linear and similar in style to the two reproduced here, the head-piece to Book I (fig. 17) and the full-page illustration to Book VI (fig. 18). They convey the impression, probably through their purity of line, that the artist has been highly successful in capturing the classical spirit and in establishing perfect harmony between text and illustrations. Christian Zervos, who analysed the work shortly after it was published,[20] also praises Picasso's flowing line, but we cannot share his view of the illustrations. We certainly disagree with his statement that 'they are not illustrations in the strict sense of the word, but entirely personal interpretations of the world which Ovid had in mind'. First of all we must object to the description of the etchings as 'entirely personal' interpretations. Of course, every artistic interpretation is entirely personal, but it is hard to believe that Zervos intended such a commonplace. If he applies this epithet to an artist of such exuberant originality as Picasso, one is led to expect something particularly idiosyncratic. In actual fact the opposite is true, for even those steeped in the academic tradition will understand and appreciate these prints at first glance. Indeed it may be said that Picasso has created few other book illustrations in which his interpretation of the spirit of the text agrees so closely with that commonly accepted. Besides, Zervos's contention does not hold good for the fifteen full-page etchings, which are doubtless illustrations in the full sense — graphic representations of scenes described in the text. It is as if a spark from Ovid's great epic, which embodies for us in large measure the spirit of the antique, had kindled Picasso to forgo his frequent exaggeration of individual elements and to illustrate this book in a manner less at variance with tradition than is usual with him.

Nor can we subscribe to Zervos's opinion that Picasso had confined himself to the static elements of the poem and neglected the dynamic side, the change of forms. Such a view seems to us to be superficial and not to do justice to the artist's work. Misled by the classic calm of the flowing lines, Zervos appears to have overlooked the dynamic force concealed behind it. It is true that some of the full-

19.   Headpiece to Act I of Aristophanes, *Lysistrata*, 1934. *See page 47*

20. Full-page illustration to Aristophanes, *Lysistrata*, 1934. Etching. Original size. *See page 47*

page prints (those to Books III, IV, XII, XIV and XV) are idyllic in character. But most of the others are instinct with a movement and a temperament which, far from being static, fully reflect the dynamic side of the poem. The illustration reproduced here should bear this out sufficiently (fig. 18).

In the head-pieces, however, the static element is in fact predominant. Here Picasso has pictured the world of the antique such as it appeared to his imagination — and to that of our generation.[21] This last fact is confirmed by the circumstances that led to the publication of his next illustrated book.

The commission to illustrate the *Lysistrata* of Aristophanes came from the publishers, the Limited Editions Club in New York. The illustrations were made in 1933 and 1934 (the tail-piece, in the colophon, is dated Paris, 26 Décembre XXXIII, the etching after page 103, 4 février XXXIV) and the book appeared in 1934. The Limited Editions Club is a kind of collectors' association, a publishing enterprise which by-passes the bookseller and distributes its books direct to its members. Most of its publications were then printed by a firm in Westport, Conn., which was associated with the Club, but some have been produced by other American and by important European printing firms. Nearly all its books are illustrated, but while the typography is consistently careful and elegant, the choice of the illustrations sometimes leaves room for doubt. Or rather, there can be no doubt that many of them are mediocre. It is no exaggeration to say that the *Lysistrata* illustrations are the most important which the Club has ever published.

Excepting Matisse, who illustrated Joyce's *Ulysses* for the Limited Editions Club, and Picasso, its commissions were given only to artists whose work was in the traditional or sometimes even in the academic manner. It is probable that the directors of the Club, whose taste certainly did not favour the *avant-garde*, decided to commission the *Lysistrata* illustrations from Picasso precisely because his Ovid etchings reflected so faithfully the commonly accepted idea of the antique.

The *Lysistrata* contains thirty-four pen drawings printed in red from line blocks in the text, and six full-page etchings.[22] All the illustrations are strictly linear and purely realistic. This book alone would suffice to disprove the contention of the Picasso connoisseur who denied Picasso's intention and almost his ability to illustrate, for it is quite evident that the artist had studied the play

46

closely and that he himself chose for illustration the scenes which appealed to him most. The six etchings represent: the council of the women under Lysistrata's leadership; Kinesias and Myrrhine (two prints); two desperate men on the sea-shore; the negotiations between the Athenians and the envoys from Sparta; and finally the celebration of peace and the reconciliation of the two sexes. There is little doubt that the publishers, had they been consulted, would have made an entirely different selection. The present uneven distribution of the full-page illustrations, with the first etching opposite page 42 and the five others between pages 90 and 115, certainly does not give the book that balance which in principle is to be desired. But with a sure eye Picasso has chosen the five cardinal points of the plot, and it speaks for his instinct as illustrator that he made two prints for the most delightful scene of the play. One of these, reproduced here (fig. 20), has caught to perfection the delicate nuances of the text: the woman offers resistance to her husband's desire, but she clearly finds it hard and one can feel how she is torn between her own desire, which is sharpened by her love for him, and the self-imposed duty to refuse him until peace has been concluded. These six prints are serious, just as the play has, fundamentally, a very serious message. But it is a comedy, for all that, and Aristophanes's humour and satire find their counterpart in Picasso's pen drawings. The head of Lysistrata at the beginning of the first Act (fig. 19) is no more than the noble profile of a determined woman, but most of the other drawings show decided touches of caricature. His warriors are helmeted fools — it is not easy to express so much folly in so few lines — his senators, like those in the play, are cunning rogues, and his crowds and combat scenes partake of that Homeric tumultuousness which never fails to amuse the twentieth-century reader (figs. 21–24).

Barr describes the *Lysistrata* illustrations as the most important made by Picasso in the 1930's and adds expressly that they come nearer to following the text than any of his earlier book illustrations.[23] We agree with Barr, though we except the full-page etchings to the *Métamorphoses*, of which the same is true.

Boeck must have been particularly impressed by the illustrations to Ovid and Aristophanes, for they are the only ones he mentions in his extensive book on Picasso.[24] In writing of the classicistic element in the artist's oeuvre he says that this art 'reached its culmination in the etchings to Ovid's *Metamorphoses*, in which the purity of line, the economy of detail and the balance of the composi-

21.   Half-page illustration to Aristophanes, *Lysistrata*, 1934.
Line-block after a pen drawing. 145 × 185 mm. *See page 47*

22. Text illustration to Aristophanes, *Lysistrata*, 1934.
Line-block after a pen drawing. Original size. *See page 47*

KINESIAS: The sentinel? Oh, Zeus, a woman soldier! *(Changes to friendlier tone, as one soldier addressing another)* Now listen, brother, I'm a soldier too. Here, I'll stand duty for you. Go call Myrrhina.

LYSISTRATA: Why should I call Myrrhina? Is she your sister?

KINESIAS: Thank Zeus she's not. *(Proudly)* I'm her husband, Kinesias.

LYSISTRATA: Well, good day, Kinesias. I've heard a lot about you. Almost too much. Myrrhina's always saying, "Kinesias dotes on pears" or "Kinesias is so bright."

**Act II
Page 85**

23. A page from Aristophanes, *Lysistrata*, 1934. *See page 47.*
Line-block after a pen drawing.

Copy number

1436

of this edition of

L Y S I S T R A T A

*Fifteen hundred copies were printed
for members of The Limited Editions
Club from the etchings and drawings
made exclusively for this edition by
Pablo Picasso, who signs this copy:*

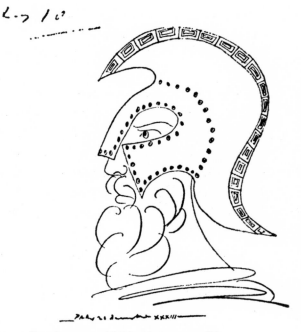

*This edition has been designed by George
Macy and printed, in Caslon types on
Rives paper, at The Printing-Office of
The Limited Editions Club, Westport,
Connecticut: Julian E. Berla, manager;
John F. McNamara, pressman;
John T. Logan, stoneman.*

24.   The last page from Aristophanes, *Lysistrata*, 1934. *See page 47.*
Line-block after a pen drawing.

tion approach the limits of perfection. In the etchings to the *Lysistrata* of Aristophanes the reserve towards the subject and the purely linear balance have given way to a stronger decorative emphasis.'

These three books, *Le Chef-d'œuvre inconnu*, the *Métamorphoses*, and the *Lysistrata*, exhausted Picasso's contacts with works of great literature for a long time to come. Nearly fifteen years were to pass until he began once more to illustrate literary classics. In the meantime he contributed to a number of books written by contemporary authors, most of them personal friends.

Two of these books appeared in 1936: poems by Paul Eluard, entitled *La Barre d'appui* and *Les Yeux fertiles*. Picasso's method of making the illustrations to the former has been described by Sabartés:[25] 'He took a copper-plate measuring 215 × 315 mm., drew two lines crosswise to divide it into four equal parts, and filled the first quarter with a very complicated drawing. In the second quarter he sketched a portrait of Nusch (Eluard's wife) and in another moment he had finished the third, drawing the head of a sleeping woman with a landscape in the background. One quarter was still blank, so he daubed his palm with paint and pressed it on the copper. Before the plate was cut into four parts, 13 impressions were taken from the aquatint plate containing the three illustrations and the imprint of the artist's hand.' The impression from the uncut copper plate is reproduced here (fig. 25). After the plate had been cut, the three etchings were printed separately and appear in the book as independent prints. It goes without saying that they have no connection whatever with the text.

The edition of *La Barre d'appui*, a cycle of poems, was limited to forty copies. Only a few months later (the colophon is dated October 15, 1936), *Les Yeux fertiles*, of which *La Barre d'appui* forms the first part, came out in an edition of 1500 numbered copies. As Eluard was then still little known, this was in fact an ordinary edition and was numbered solely to mark it, in accordance with French custom, as the official first edition (*édition originale*). Of the four line blocks in this volume, three are simply reproductions of the etchings from *La Barre d'appui*, the fourth is a facsimile of Eluard's handwriting with marginal drawings by Picasso (fig. 26). Here it is clear how the artist was inspired by the poem: the female nude is the real illustration, whereas the peculiar head at the left and the cubist shapes below paraphrase the at once uncanny and frivolous

52

25.   Three illustrations to Paul Eluard, *La Barre d'Appui*, 1936.
Etching. Impression from the uncut plate; in the lower left quarter an
impression of Picasso's hand which was not reproduced in the book.
315 × 215 mm. *See page 52*

26. Illustration to Paul Eluard, *Les Yeux fertiles*, 1936. Line-block after a pen drawing. This illustration is in the same size as that in Eluard's book. The original drawing is larger. *See page 52*

27. Illustration to Iliazd, *Afat*, 1940. Etching, 250 × 146 mm. *See page 54*

28. The Cat. From Buffon, 1942. Etching. 270 × 206 mm. without lettering. *See page 54*

atmosphere of the poem. A special edition of ten copies contains a further etching by Picasso, which is quite unrelated to the text.

At this point we must mention a book that was in fact never published. In 1939 Picasso worked frequently at the gravure printing press of Lacourière. He experimented with colour gravure printing and for three months occupied himself with the project of printing his own writings with marginal drawings in colour. According to the detailed account of Sabartés,[26] Picasso's first idea was to make only a small edition of a few prints for his personal friends, but later he intended to print everything he had ever written, regardless of length, and Vollard was to publish it. In the end the whole plan was dropped and, if Sabartés is to be believed, Picasso had never been in earnest, but had amused himself with making these experiments. No such prints have ever been published and we can only record the facts, which are evidence of Picasso's literary interests in his riper years—interests that went beyond his occasional poetry, some of which has appeared, in French, in the *Cahiers d'Art*.[27] The facsimile of one poem, printed in 1938, may give some idea of the book that the artist had visualized. His dramatic poetry will be mentioned below.

War had already broken out when Iliazd (his real name is Ilja Zdanevič) published his first book, with four etchings by Picasso. A Russian émigré, he is a friend of Picasso's and writes poetry in Russian. His verses are expressionist (an idiom discouraged by the Communist régime and consequently not used by writers living in Russia) and reveal undoubted poetic gifts. Iliazd is also a passionate lover of book design, who sets his own texts in order to have full scope for realizing his typographical principles; and if these principles differ at times from our own, his unselfish devotion to the cause of the book and his sometimes highly original ideas must always command our respect.

The seventy-six sonnets, which he collected under the title *Afat*, were published in an edition limited to fifty copies. The title, which is explained in two imprints, one in Russian and the other in French, is an Arabic word meaning unhappiness or the beauty who inspires unhappy love. The imprint also records that the etchings were printed from the 4th to the 8th of December 1939 (the Russian has, 4th to 6th December, probably erroneously), the text between the 2nd and the 30th March, 1940.

Of the four prints, two are dated May 28, 1938, the third June 2, 1938, and the last, June 19, 1938. The fact that they were made almost two years before the book was published does not in itself rule out a connection with the sonnets, for these may have been written even earlier. But if we consider that Picasso does not know Russian, and that it is hard to imagine an artist illustrating poems which he cannot read, we shall not be surprised that there is no connection at all. Picasso made two further etchings specially for the book (between June 19 and June 23, 1939, according to the imprint): two Arabic words in Cufic calligraphy, 'Afat' and 'Madjusija' (sorceress). But all six copper plates are of equal size (145 mm. high and 245 mm. wide) and correspond to the oblong format of the book (200 × 300 mm.), with two sonnets placed side by side on each page.

Of the four etchings one represents a sleeping woman, the second a man with a harpy, and each of the two others a man with a reclining woman.[28] Only the last print, which is reproduced here (fig. 27), shows etched tones, the other three are wholly linear. But notwithstanding the classical purity of their lines, they differ strikingly in their expressive values from the true illustrations which Picasso had made to Ovid and Aristophanes.

By chance one of Picasso's most important graphic works was published during the war: the thirty-one etchings to the work by Buffon, the eighteenth-century French naturalist, which, though quite obsolete scientifically, is still looked upon in France as a classic of French literature. Vollard had planned this publication with Picasso many years earlier. According to Sabartés, the artist began work on the etchings in 1936, long after he had promised them to Vollard.[29] When he was in full swing, Sabartés adds, he made one etching a day. But when Vollard died in 1939, on the eve of the second World War, the book had not appeared, and another three years were to pass until Martin Fabiani was able to publish the eagerly awaited volume.

Picasso made thirty-one etchings: horse, ass, bull (twice), ram, cat (fig. 28), dog, goat, hind, wolf, lioness, monkey, eagle, vulture, sparrow-hawk, ostrich, cock, hen, turkey, pigeon, goldfinch, bee, butterfly, wasp, lobster, spider, dragonfly, lizard, toad, frog and grasshopper (fig. 29). This is not the place to analyse the high artistic value of the illustrations, but we are concerned here with the book as a whole.

According to Sabartés,[30] Vollard had given Picasso a free hand in his work. The artist took into consideration at least the basic demands of a publication in

LASAUTEKELLE

29.   The Grasshopper. From Buffon, 1942. Etching. 278 × 208 mm.
without lettering. *See page 54*

30.   Frontispiece to Georges Hugnet, *La Chèvre-feuille*, 1943. Zinc engraving.
276 × 220 mm. Impression from the first state on the gravure press.
See page 59

31. *La Chèvre-feuille*, 1943. Impression from the reworked plate on the letterpress machine. *See page 59*

32. Title page of Ramon Reventós, *Deux Contes*, 1947. Lithograph, 290 × 189 mm. *See page 66.*

book form in so far as he kept the plates fairly uniform in size. The largest, the wolf, is 350 × 250 mm., the two smallest, lioness and toad, are 267 × 210 mm., and the page size of 367 × 277 mm. is therefore just sufficient for the largest and well proportioned to the smaller plates. Picasso did not have to adapt his work to Buffon's text, but the publisher later extracted the passages treating of the animals depicted. Some of these, e.g. the horse, were given eight pages of text, others, such as the vulture, only a page and a half. With the birds the text comes to an end, and the last ten prints have no text at all, but only a fly-title in type. It is not known whether this economy was due to war conditions or had other reasons.

Rather than an illustrated book, we have here, in effect, a suite of etchings, not published in loose sheets, but coupled with letterpress taken from a classic text. The publisher has thus reversed a procedure which is frequently adopted, though generally with questionable results: instead of inserting illustrations into an important text, he has added text matter to an important work of graphic art. This was not, however, an innovation, but on the contrary a return to the starting-point of the illustrated printed book, as represented by wood-block prints (*Biblia pauperum, Defensorium inviolatae virginis Mariae,* and others) — pictorial sequences with short captions. This practice was continued through the centuries, from Dürer and Holbein to Doré, Toulouse-Lautrec and Kubin. And just as the *Métamorphoses* of Ovid with the woodcuts of Bernard Salomon (Lyons 1557) strikes us as a beautiful book although no more barbaric text could be imagined than an adaptation in bad *ottave rime,* by a mediocre poet, of the passages illustrated, so we cannot but admire and enjoy the *Buffon* of Picasso in spite of our objections to the text.[31]

The books to be considered next were also published during the war. Under the title *Divers poèmes du livre ouvert,* Eluard wrote out fifteen autograph copies of twenty pages of his poetry. These 300 sheets, dated April 18, 1941, were 'illuminated' by Picasso, that is to say, he decorated them with coloured spots. A few years later, he was to use lithography for this type of book decoration.

In the years 1942 and 1943 appeared two volumes of poems by Georges Hugnet, *Non vouloir,* with four 'gravures' and *La Chèvre-feuille,* with six 'gravures'. Picasso employed here the unusual technique of engraving the illustrations directly on the zinc plates, from which they were then printed on an ordinary press. The prints may therefore be regarded as works of original

33.   Illustration to Georges Hugnet, *Non vouloir*. 1942.
Zinc engraving (autograph zinc drawing).
Original size. *See page 57*

graphic art,[32] like woodcuts, with which the four illustrations to *Non vouloir* have much in common. This is a case which shows clearly how hard it is sometimes to distinguish between real illustrations and prints added more or less at random. That Picasso engraved the zinc plates specially for this volume is beyond doubt. Two of them are reproduced here. The first (fig. 33) is placed opposite the following poem:

> *Tête sans tête*
> *Bras sans bras*
> *Qui caracole dans le noir?*
>
> *Tout fantôme*
> *N'emporte pas qui veut*
> *D'une armure dans l'autre.*

It would not be a rash assumption that Picasso was inspired by this poem to create his phantom, and the print even suggests the 'caracoler dans le noir', to the point of expressing the double meaning of *noir* as blackness and darkness. And yet — who can tell whether the artist did not draw the figure spontaneously from the zinc surface in front of him, long before the author or the publisher found how well it matched the poem and placed it on the opposite page?

The second illustration (fig. 34) accompanies the poem on p. 48;

> *Euphorie ô ma douceur*
> *Sphinx étroit tu intéresses*
> *A travers tant de maîtresses*
> *Tout l'amour que j'ai au cœur.*
>
> *C'est l'amour toujours pareil*
> *Et jamais indispensable*
> *Qui coule comme le sable*
> *Entre deux doigts de soleil.*

The lines express the resignation of a man who sees perfection in every woman and each time finds himself disappointed, because all he really seeks is a proof of his own capability to love — in brief, the old problem of Don Juan. On the

34. Illustration to Georges Hugnet, *Non Vouloir*. 1942.
Zinc engraving (autograph zinc drawing). Original size.
See page 57

opposite page we have the cubist construction of a woman's body, and again the question arises whether Picasso constructed his Venus for this particular poem or simply used the zinc plate for a quite independent conception of a female figure. Either alternative is possible, but a precise knowledge of how the print originated is of secondary importance for an appreciation of the final result. In either case we have here a true illustration, which has all the qualities that can fairly be expected. The same could be shown for the other two 'autograph zinc drawings', but the corresponding poems are much more hermetic and so ambiguous in their connotations that their interpretation would itself be open to doubts.

La Chèvre-feuille is a cycle of love poems addressed to a woman whom the poet calls Viviane. Here Picasso employed a different technique. For *Non vouloir* he had worked in large areas from black to white as if engraving on wood, now he incised purely linear drawings into the six zinc plates. The *édition de luxe* (25 copies out of a total of 550) contains an 'etching', which is nothing else but an impression from one of the zinc plates taken on the gravure press before it was prepared for the letterpress machine. Both prints are reproduced here. In the 'etching' (fig. 30) the lines left open appear in white on black ground, in the relief print (fig. 31) as black key drawing. After the twenty-five gravure prints had been made, the zinc plate was further treated with the graver and other instruments, thus producing the screenlike hatching and the white lines and areas. Picasso did not show much regard for the text, but has drawn women's bodies and heads which would go equally well with any other love poems as with those of Hugnet. Special mention should be made of the first illustration, representing thirteen female heads placed irregularly on a background shaded off from deep black to light grey. This print is extraordinarily powerful and impressive both in design and in its black-and-white effect. Of both books by Hugnet there are *de luxe* editions with colour prints of the illustrations.

For the sake of completeness we must here mention a publication which does not really come within the scope of this study: *Pablo Picasso, Grâce et mouvement, 14 compositions originales gravées sur cuivre*, published in 1943 by Louis Grosclaude in Zürich. The publisher had fourteen drawings of dance scenes by Picasso transferred on to copper plates and printed them together with fourteen Sapphic odes which he selected on his own account and, as he admits, without

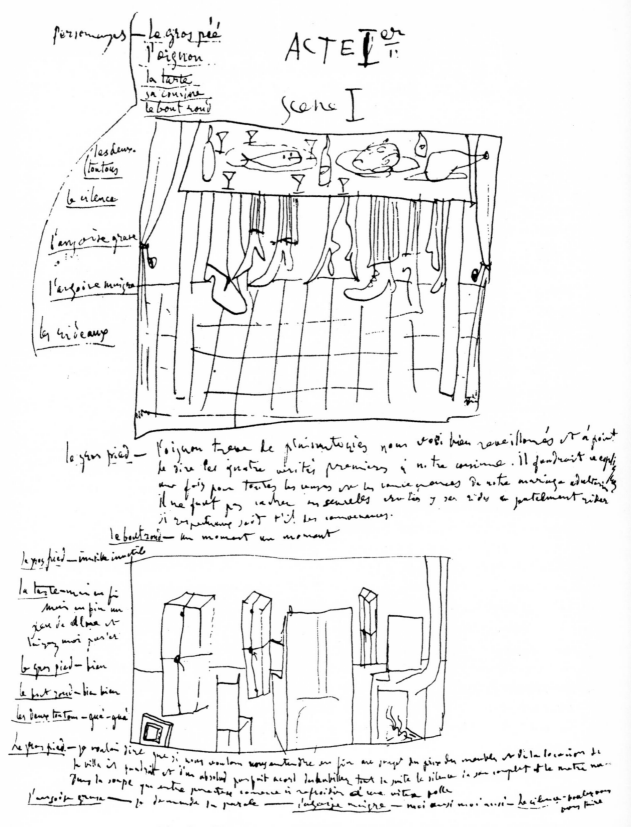

35–36.   First pages of Picasso's *Le Désir attrapé par la queue*, written in 194

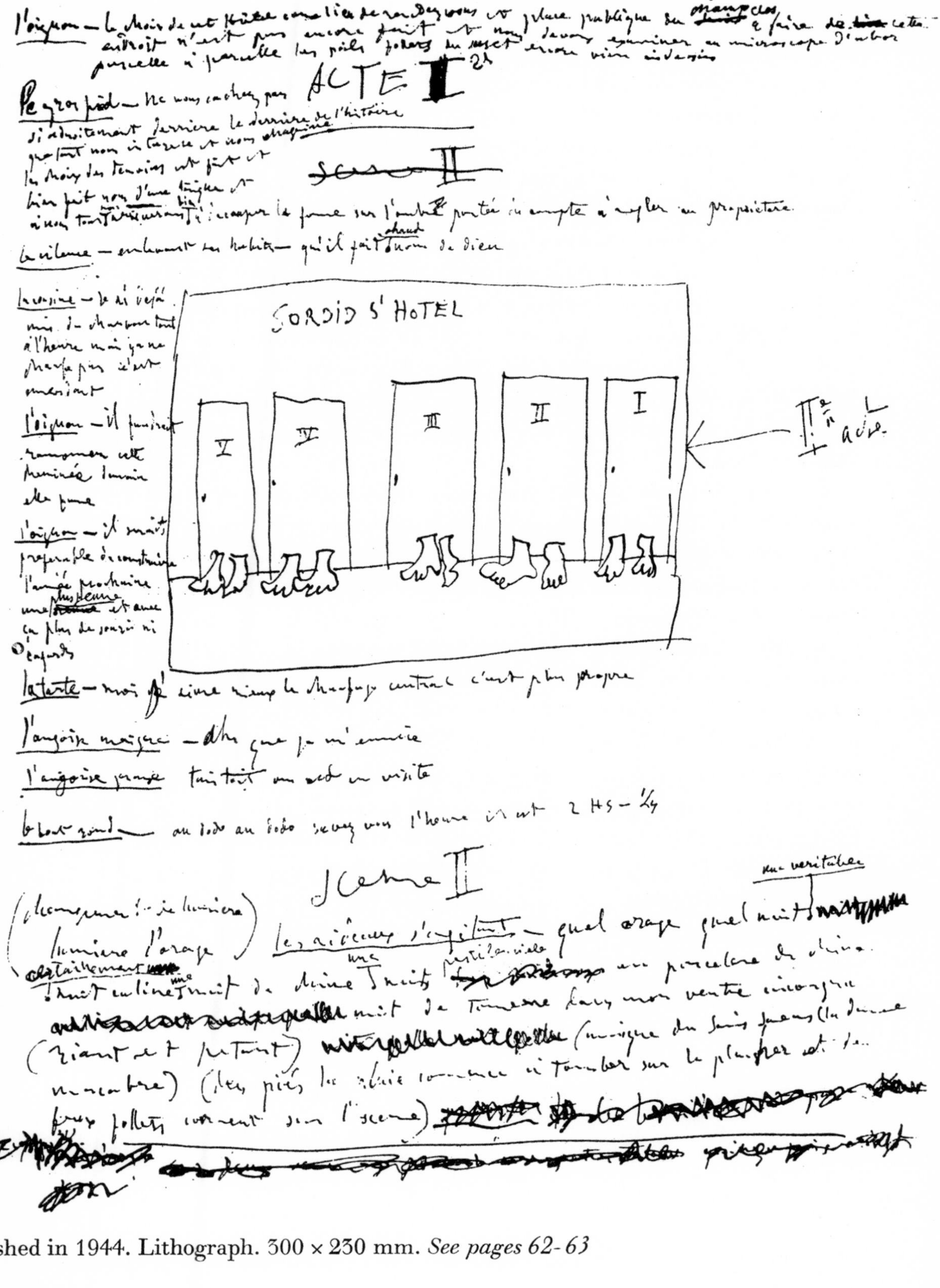

ACTE I

SCÈNE II

SORDID S' HOTEL

V   IV   III   II   I

Scène II

reference to the drawings. His somewhat grandiloquent and self-satisfied preface cannot dispel the impression that the publication was designed to tempt the undiscriminating collector.[83]

The next book, also more curious than important, was a collection of verse by Robert Desnos, published in the summer of 1944 under the title *Contrée*. To these poems, which are written in the traditional manner, Picasso contributed an etching which fits the text neither in style nor in subject: a human figure built up of a network of lines (dated 23 D. — presumably December — 43), suggestive, to the present writer, of a fighting robot or lansquenet. Sections of this print[34] are reproduced from line blocks as tail-vignettes to 23 of the 25 poems: now a shoulder and arm, then a leg, sometimes isolated fragments which are no more than linear ornaments. Whether the artist, the author or the publisher was responsible for this idea, we cannot regard the experiment as more than a curiosity.

The war years saw also the publication of the only play which Picasso has published: *Le Désir attrapé par la queue*.[35] He began writing it on January 14, 1941, and completed it three days later, but as it was wholly surrealist it could not be printed during the German occupation of Paris and appeared for the first time in 1944. This edition (believed to be only between 30 and 40 copies), a photo-litho reproduction of the manuscript, deserves to be described in some detail if only because of its rarity. It is a sketch-book measuring 315 × 235 mm., consisting of a cover and twelve leaves. The front cover has a drawing designed by the firm which distributes the sketch-book: the word 'Dessin' in pedantic calligraphy, running upwards diagonally over the full width, and two shell-like ornaments placed unsymmetrically above and below. The cover as a whole looks indescribably bizarre in its unmistakable imitation Baroque of the 1880's. On the inside of the front cover Picasso has inscribed the starting date 'Paris mardi 14 janvier 1941' and the title. Opposite (on fol. 1 recto) there is a full-page self-portrait of the artist.[36] The following two pages (fol. 1 verso and 2 recto) are blank, that on the left being reserved for the date of dedication, that on the right for the owner's name, both in Picasso's hand, and his signature. The text begins on fol. 2 verso with a list of characters and the first Act. On the same page there are two drawings (fig. 35) and on the opposite page is a third drawing (fig. 36), but this refers to the second Act, which starts overleaf on fol. 3

verso. Act IV also starts with a drawing, on fol. 7 recto. At the bottom of fol. 12 verso the text ends with the words 'Fin de la pièce Paris vendredi 17 janvier 1941'; the back cover is blank. In the copy which we have examined the dedication is dated 'Paris 25 mars 1944'.

In May 1944 the play was read before an invited audience at the Galerie Leiris in Paris and soon afterwards it was printed in a periodical[37] and so made known to a wider public. In 1945 it was published by the well-known firm of Gallimard as a slender booklet, in which the self-portrait was used as frontispiece in much reduced size and three drawings were reproduced from line blocks as headpieces to the first, second and fourth Acts, the second text illustration of the facsimile edition being omitted.

The first scene, a visit to 'Big Foot' on New Year's Eve, opens with a drawing of ingenious composition: the front of a table laden with food and drink, and five pairs of legs dangling underneath. The action of the second Act takes place in 'Sordid's Hotel', which is represented by a corridor with five closed doors and before each, instead of shoes, a pair of chopped-off feet. The fourth Act has only one scene, in which each of the characters announces that he has won the jackpot in a lottery; it is illustrated with a rapid sketch of a few figures seated round a dial-like roulette wheel. The drawings, with their rectangular borders, are reminiscent of first sketches for stage designs. They are scurrilous caricatures in the spirit of the play, and even the self-portrait of the artist at work seen from above is grotesquely humorous.

Apollinaire's *Les Mamelles de Tirésias*, of 1946, contains six reproductions after drawings by Picasso. All are portrait caricatures of the poet and not illustrations of the text.[38]

If the etched frontispiece to *Contrée* was remarkable for the peculiar use to which it was put in the book, the frontispiece to another book deserves to be mentioned on its own account. In 1947 an anonymous private amateur (it was Louis Aragon) published privately five of Petrarch's sonnets to Laura with French translations by himself and a short introduction. (His motto: 'They said Laura was somebody Else' suggests that the book was intended for his wife Elsa Triolet.) A Picasso etching of a beautiful woman's head forms an exquisite decoration.[39] As the etching is dated January 9, 1945, it can reasonably be assumed to have been made quite independently. But it is in no way discordant

37. Illustration to Ramon Reventós, *Dos Contes*, 1947. Etching.
304 × 254 mm. *See page 66.*

38.   Illustration to Ramon Reventós, *Deux Contes*, 1947. Etching.
300 × 242 mm. *See page 66.*

E

and the book as a whole is so well produced that the recipients had every reason to be delighted with it.

After Hugnet's *La Chèvre-feuille* of December 1943 no book with autograph prints by Picasso appeared for almost three and a half years. The next was published in the spring of 1947: *Dos Contes*, two tales in the Catalan language, by Ramon Reventós, a friend from Picasso's early years. A French translation, published in the summer of the same year, is identical in design, and so we can discuss both editions together. The two stories have a slightly ironical flavour. In the first, a Catalan takes into his employment a Centaur, with whom he passes through various adventures until he finds the right job for him — as tutor to his children. The second tale is about a faun, the sole survivor from antiquity, who emigrates to Spain, where he carries on all manner of activities: as pedlar of groundnuts, artist's model, municipal park keeper, goatherd, and finally variety artist. At this stage he falls in love with a woman, but when he finds himself deceived by her he returns to the forest and dies.

For both books Picasso lettered the title-pages, fly-titles and binding as well as the initials (one for each paragraph), which were printed in lithography; he also made eight etchings (four for the French and four for the Catalan edition), so that all printing processes are used in the same book: relief, intaglio and planographic. All his initials and lettered pages are in the same style as the title-page of the French edition reproduced here (fig. 32). For the story of the Centaur in the Catalan edition Picasso etched a page of scenes from the life of the Centaur and his master (fig. 37); a second print is divided into three parts, showing the Centaur as picador, harnessed to a peasant cart, and as tutor[40] (both etchings are dated: February 4 and 5, 1947). For the French edition he preferred to make two etchings of large figures: the Centaur with the cart, and as picador (fig. 38). For the story of the Faun in the Catalan edition he etched a large faun playing a double flute and another print divided into three scenes, showing the faun fighting a buck, as artist's model, and dying (dated February 5 and 6, 1947); the French edition has another version of the flute-playing faun and also a quite different version of the dying faun.[41] The etchings are illustrations in the strict sense of the word. Like the two tales, they are not of great moment, but spirited and attractive. The typography of the book, however, is not so successful. It is set in a large size (24 or perhaps even 30 point) of a very thin sans-serif type, which contrasts too much with the broad brushstrokes of Picasso's titles and initials. Such a text page with wide margins and over-fat initials on the left and an etching which bleeds off at the right do not make a well-balanced opening. The binding is also somewhat unsatisfactory: thick wood boards of natural colour with a narrow red leather spine and red lettering.

The following year, 1948, was particularly fruitful. First, brief mention should be made of an unusual book, *La Vie est sans pitié* by Pierre Bettencourt, containing eleven short stories which could be described, if we adapt the title of a volume of poems well known forty years ago,[42] as 'Tales of an unfeeling Heart'. The book was printed, in an edition of 101 numbered copies, on the author's press at Saint-Maurice d'Etelan, and the presswork is beautiful, though perhaps a little too black. The cover has a reproduction of an etching by Picasso, representing a man with a bull's head, his hand raised high and holding a two-edged poniard — a symbol very appropriate to the text. The etching is one of the Minotaur series of 1933 and had already been reproduced in the first issue of the periodical *Minotaure* (opposite page 1). We have here another proof that a work of graphic art may have been made quite independently of a text and may yet illustrate it extremely well; the opposite is also true, as we have seen in some of the books discussed before.

The most important publication of 1948 was the *Gongora*, one of the greatest of Picasso's books. If the illustrations to *Lysistrata* showed us in which way the artist carried out a commission coming to him from without, the *Gongora* must have been a text which Picasso, as a native of Spain, had close at heart.

Luis de Gongora, the poet of the Spanish Baroque (1561–1627), has rarely been translated into other languages and is therefore little known to those who cannot read his work in the original. In Spain he is regarded as one of the great national poets, and lovers of Spanish poetry are full of enthusiasm for his verses. Picasso has chosen twenty of Gongora's sonnets, for which he made twenty pairs of etchings, with an additional title etching of the poet's signature. One plate of each pair has the text of a sonnet etched in dry-point with marginal drawings, the other has a head inspired by the poem. Of all books which Picasso has illustrated, the *Gongora* is one of the present writer's favourites and he would have liked to reproduce here all the heads with the corresponding sonnets. However, we must limit ourselves to two examples.[43]

Sonnet XVIII (fig. 39) praises the charms of a young girl gathering flowers. We can see that Picasso made no attempt to imitate professional calligraphy: he simply wrote the text down as he might have written an urgent letter, he even made a few mistakes and left some of them uncorrected. Yet the page as a whole has a fascination which defies analysis and which only those ignorant of Latin characters could enjoy to the full. A sensitive Arab or Chinese not acquainted with the Western alphabet would judge such a page better than we do. But if we are able to look at it fixedly until the meaning of the letters is effaced and only the interplay of lines and curves remains, then the beauty of the black-and-white pattern will begin to emerge and to fascinate us irresistibly, like interlaced Arabic calligraphy, whose poetic meaning remains hidden from us. . . . The handwriting which we know from the letter to Reventós of 1900 and from the awkward attempt on the Stravinsky cover of 1919 has here reached its prime. At the age of sixty-six, the artist has brought to maturity the fruit that lay budding in the youth of nineteen.

The head which we reproduce (fig. 40) belongs to Sonnet VII, entitled 'On the Death of Dona Guiomar de Sa, wife of Juan Fernandez de Espinosa'. We quote this marvellously tender poem in full, with a plain, almost literal prose translation, which cannot, of course, reproduce the play on the names Sa and Espinosa in the original.

Palida restituya a su elemento
Su ya esplendor purpureo, casta rosa,
Que en planta, dulce un tiempo, si espinosa,
Gloria del Sol, lisonja fue del viento.

El mismo que espiro, suave aliento,
Fresca, espira marchota y siempre hermosa,
No yace, no, en la tierra, mas remosa,
Negandole aun al hado lo violento.

Sus hojas si, no su fragranzia, llora
En polvo el patrio Betis, hojas bellas,
Que aun el polvo el materno Tajo dora

39. Text page with marginal drawings from *Gongora*, 1948. Etching.
350 × 243 mm. *See page 68*

40.   Illustration to *Gongora*, 1948. Etching. 335 × 220 mm.
See pages 68–69

Introduction

Ya en nuevos campos una es oy de aquellas
Flores, que ilustra otra mejor Aurora
Cuyo caduco aljofar son estrellas.

Pale she restores to her element
her already purple splendour, the chaste rose,
which on her bush, sweet for a while, though thorny,
was the glory of the sun, the delight of the wind.

The same sweet fragrance which she exhaled
Fresh, she exhales faded and still beautiful,
she lies not in the earth, no, but she rests,
depriving even fate of its violence.

Her leaves, not her fragrance laments,
now she is dust, father Betis, the lovely leaves,
which even as dust the maternal Tajo gilds.

Already in new fields she is today one of those
flowers which another, better dawn lights up
whose transient jewels are the stars.

We need hardly draw attention to the exquisite delicacy of the woman's head
which stands opposite this sonnet, and it matters little whether Picasso was in
fact inspired by the poem to make his etching or had already made the sketch
and then chose it to accompany the poem. When we see the sonnet and the
print side by side we feel that they are in perfect harmony — and that is all
that matters.

The book is made up as follows: after the etched title-page — a facsimile of
Gongora's signature — and the preliminary pages in letterpress, each sonnet has
first a fly-title in French, then the head, then the etched Spanish text with the
marginal drawings, and finally the French prose translation by Zdislas Milner
(the French prefer to translate foreign poetry in prose). In this way, the *Gongora*
has been cast in the form of a book, although it is essentially a suite of etchings.
The illustrative character of the book is not thereby impaired. The paper was

specially made and Picasso has designed a watermark, which is beautiful and in harmony with the material (fig. 41).

41.   Watermark designed by Picasso for *Gongora*, 1948.

The *de luxe* copies (Nos. 1–15) contain a suite of all the etchings on Japanese or Chinese paper, and these prints — except for one sonnet and two heads — are dated on the plate. This gives us an interesting insight into the progress of the work. On February 26 and 27, 1947, Picasso etched seven heads, including the portrait of Gongora[44] — a stupendous and almost incredible feat. After an interval of well over three months, he continued in June: the first text page was finished on the 12th, two further text pages and one head on the 18th, one text page on the 19th, three on the 25th and another on the 26th, a text page and five heads on the 29th, another text page on July 1st and two more on July 2nd. The greater part of the work was now finished, but seven full months were to pass before the artist resumed work. On February 4, 1948, he made three text pages and four heads, and two days later, on February 6th, he made the last three text pages, which completed the work. On March 9th he drew Gongora's signature for the title-page.

Picasso used here a very unusual technique, the sugar aquatint. This has been described in great detail by John Buckland-Wright and we refer the

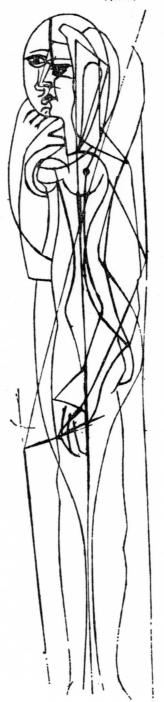

42. Illustration from Iliazd, *Pis'mo*, 1948. Etching.
Size of the plate 330 × 64 mm. *See page 72*

reader to his excellent discussion, which is accompanied by twelve reproductions.[45]

In the same year the poet Iliazd, whose volume of sonnets has been discussed above, printed a lengthy poem entitled *Pis'mo* (The Letter). This book, like other Iliazd books illustrated by Picasso, has a most unorthodox lay-out. It consists of twelve pages, each containing six stanzas of four lines. The type area is about 215 mm. deep and 80 mm. wide, the size of the book is 365 × 240 mm. The type area is therefore much too narrow for the normal page, but the sheets have been folded in such a way that only some of the pages have the full width of the book, while the others vary in width between 85 and 160 mm. Picasso has contributed four etchings, all of them 330 mm. deep, but varying in width. The title etching has a total width of 205 mm., but the female nude seen from the back, which extends over the whole depth and is placed near the foredge, is only 50 mm. wide, while the rest of the plate contains merely the title PIS'MO written by Picasso in Cyrillic capitals in the optical centre; in the lower half of the plate the word is repeated upside down and struck out.[46] The same plate was printed also on a parchment sheet, which serves as cover. Of the other plates, two are about 140 mm. wide and the last only 64 mm. (like a fifth plate, which was rejected). In addition there is a sixth print, an impression taken from the same plate that was later used for one of the etchings of 140 mm. width. This sixth print was made when the plate had still its original width of 205 mm. (like the title etching), and one third of the space, on the right, is taken up by an intricate system of interlaced curves, which was cut off before the actual book illustration was printed. The poem is dated 1946, of the etchings three are dated March 3, 1947, one March 14, 1947 (rejected) and one April 14, 1947. All represent female nudes (fig. 42) and have no connection with the text, an epistle addressed to a beloved woman in a spirit of resignation.

The edition was limited to fifty numbered copies printed on Japanese paper. The imprint proper is in Spanish, the limitation certificate (*justification du tirage*), signed by the poet and by the artist, in Russian, running up the page and concluded by the line 'Tous droits réservés pour tous pays copyright by Iliazd 1948'. Thus we have the result, probably unique in other than multilingual bibliophile books, that four different languages are used on two pages.

Another book published in the same year also belongs among the curiosities. During the war Pierre Reverdy had written a cycle of forty-three poems, *Le*

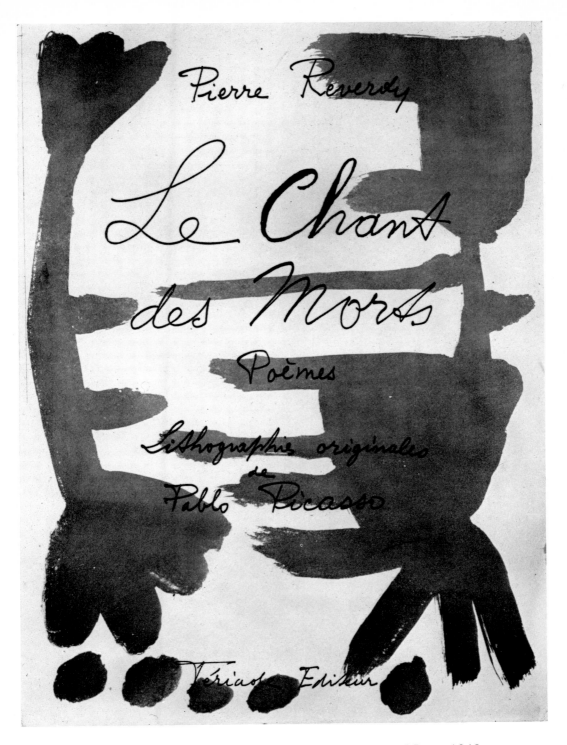

43. Title page of Pierre Reverdy, *Le Chant des Morts*, 1948.
Lithograph in black with red 'illuminations'. 410 × 308 mm.
Mourlot, *Picasso lithographe* II, 73. *See page 73*

44.   Illustration from Iwan Goll, *Elégie d'Iphétonga*, 1949.
Lithograph. 300 × 200 mm. *See page 75*

Chant des morts, which he finished on January 5, 1945. More than three and a half years later his manuscript was published in facsimile by the firm of Tériade, with lithographs contributed by Picasso. These lithographs, printed in red, are intended only as illuminations. On every page, distributed irregularly, there are stripes, spots and circles, which have exactly the same function as the work of miniaturists (artists applying minium or red lead) in medieval manuscripts. The result is a repetition, in lithography, of what Picasso had done by hand in 1941 for the poems of Eluard. The title-page, reproduced here (fig. 43), gives a good idea of this manner of decoration, if it is borne in mind that only the handwriting is in black and everything else in bright red. The book is a large folio (420 × 325 mm.), the minuscules are up to 11 mm. high (not reckoning ascenders and descenders) and the 'illuminations' make a somewhat barbaric and violent impression.

But there is also another way of looking at this work. One critic, whose views on art lean towards the traditional rather than the revolutionary, was so much impressed by the book that he wrote: 'However strange the illustrations to *Le Chant des morts* may appear at first sight, they are soon found to be neither cheap nor extravagant. The autograph text, which Reverdy had completed on January 5, 1945, is reproduced in facsimile in a folio volume. Texts of suffering, misery and hope from the days when the poet endured the servitude of the Occupation in Solesmes. Picasso deals with this text in the manner of medieval miniators, who filled the margins of their fine parchments with fruit and flowers whose decorative value does not exclude symbolic character. But Picasso is a miniator who has lived through the cubist revolution and swims on the tide of the Surrealism of his time. The traditional forms of another epoch could not appeal to him. He took his brush, dipped it into lithographic ink and drew on the stone broad vertical and horizontal stripes, circles, flames, schematic wings and curves which, like bent dumb-bells, run into circular masses. . . . This entire geometry is printed in a vivid red, it frames the pages, runs across them, articulates them, emphasizes them, as if a stream of blood — the blood of the dead — had poured forth over the sheets. And more than that: all the graphisms which surround the text like an inexorable menace here become the condensed forms of unseen instruments which oppress, torture, pierce, and thus take on the significance of tragic symbols.'[47]

'avais toujours soupçonné les géographes de ne savoir ce qu'ils disent lorsqu'ils placent le champ de bataille de Munda dans le pays des Bastuli-Pœni, près de la moderne Monda, à quelque deux lieues au nord de Marbella. D'après mes propres conjectures sur le texte de l'anonyme, auteur du *Bellum Hispaniense*, et quelques renseignements recueillis dans l'excellente bibliothèque du duc d'Ossuna, je pensais qu'il fallait chercher aux environs de Montilla le lieu mémorable où, pour la dernière fois, César joua quitte ou double contre les champions de la république. Me trouvant en Andalousie au commencement de l'automne de 1830, je fis une assez longue excursion pour éclaircir les doutes qui me restaient encore. Un mémoire que je publierai prochainement ne laissera plus, je l'espère, aucune incertitude dans l'esprit de tous les archéologues de bonne foi. En attendant que ma dissertation

13

45.   Initial letter from Mérimée, *Carmen*, 1949. Etching. *See page 75*

Introduction

Three books with contributions by Picasso appeared in 1949. The author of the first was Yvan Goll, an expressionist who had written German poetry in the 1920's and had then moved to Paris, where he began to write in French. During the second World War he lived in New York and after his return to Paris he worked up his American impressions into a poem of ten short cantos, the *Elégie d'Iphétonga* — the latter an old Red Indian name for a district which is today a part of Brooklyn. The Elegy is followed by a group of seven poems under the heading *Masques de cendre*. Picasso contributed four lithographs, three of devils' faces[48] and one of a strange, somewhat uncanny female head *en face* — all dated April 11, 1949. The high quality of the lithographs does not alter the fact that they have nothing in common with the poems — unless the devils and the head are identified with the *Masques* of the title (fig. 44).

This applies even more to the edition of Mérimée's immortal *Carmen* published in the same year. One might have expected that the Spanish theme would have interested the artist, but that was not the case. The thirty full-page linear etchings represent nothing but faces — not imaginary portraits of characters in the story, but just faces. It is revealing, interesting and sometimes even exciting to observe Picasso's virtuosity in these variations on the eternal theme of the human face (fig. 46), and some of the prints are superb; but they have no connection whatever with Mérimée. The Spanish head-dress of the frontispiece (fig. 47) might conceivably suggest Carmen, but even that would be far-fetched. The etchings which Picasso made specially for this book are the initials and tail-ornaments for each of the four chapters (fig. 45).

The third book published in 1949 is yet another curiosity, a collection of twenty-one 'poems' and twenty-three prints edited by Iliazd under the title *Poésies des mots inconnus*. It consists of five folders containing loose leaves, each with a Dadaist poem made up of non-existent words of French, German and Russian. The prints are by various modern artists, among them Matisse, Braque and Arp. Picasso's contributions are the following: a dry-point etching, very strongly stylized (Gieure calls such drawings 'ideograms'), to a poem by Pierre Albert Birot; four pages of diary notes in manuscript,[49] reproduced in lithography (these may help us to visualize the book which, according to Sabartés, Picasso was writing by hand in 1939); and finally the last item in the book, seven fantastic lines

46. Illustration from Mérimée, *Carmen*, 1949. Etching.
235 × 153 mm. *See page 75*

47. Illustration from Mérimée, Carmen, 1949. Etching.
253 × 166 mm. *See page 75*

of non-existent letters (also reproduced in lithography) ridiculing the 'mots inconnus', the unknown words.[50] This publication is also remarkable for its unorthodox typography. Iliazd himself set the type and his highly original book design is in keeping with the amusing contents.

Corps perdu, a cycle of ten poems by the Negro poet Aimé Césaire, published in 1950, is one of the most interesting books illustrated by Picasso, but also one of the most esoteric and hardest to understand. The artist has contributed thirty full-page etchings, a calligraphic drawing for the cover and the design of the watermark (fig. 48). The motto of the book reads:

> *nègre nègre nègre*
> *depuis le fond du ciel immémorial* . . .

and a Negro head serves as frontispiece (fig. 49). The details of this head are hatched with a delicacy to which no reproduction can do full justice,

48.   Watermark designed by Picasso for *Corps perdu*, 1950.

78

but even here the charm of this masterly print should prove irresistible. The realism of this head contrasts with the style of the other prints, which are ideograms, simplifications of such intense concentration that they are as hard to decipher as Césaire's poetry, which does not yield up its meaning readily.

Each poem is accompanied by three etchings. The first is an illustration with a space left in the middle for the title of the poem (one or two words), in such a way that the blank space forms a natural part of the design. It is astonishing how well the black-and-white effect of these etchings matches that of the titles. The line etchings to the text are in perfect graphic harmony with the poems, which are set in the large size of a slender Old Face, while the more painterly fly-titles correspond in colour value to the short titles of the poems, for which slightly heavier capitals not unlike Plantin have been used. The first poem, entitled 'Mot', is an ecstatic lament over the exclamation 'Negro', which breaks up the embrace. The corresponding fly-title shows a stylized head with curly hair, and it is astonishing how well the word MOT fits into the forehead; Picasso must have designed the composition with this word in mind.[51] The same applies to the other title-etchings, as the reader can judge for himself from a reproduction of the fly-title to the third poem (fig. 50). The second etching to the first poem is a strictly linear, strongly stylized erotic scene of a man and a woman, while the third is an ideogram which we are unable to interpret.[52] The second poem is entitled 'Présence'. Its fly-title shows a group of nine human figures sketched in quite primitive lines, the second print is an unmistakable ideogram of sexual union, and the third shows a crescent-shaped profile to the right, with over-lifesize eyes, and a system of hyperbolic curves on the left. As the meaning of this poem eludes us, we cannot judge of its relation to the illustrations. The third poem, entitled 'longitude', begins as follows:

Et les collines soulèvent
de leurs épaules grêles
de leurs épaules sans paille
de leurs épaules d'eau jaune de terre noire
de nénuphar torrentiel
la poitrine trois fois horrible de ciel tenace.

The title etching seems to us to do full justice to this evocation of a weird landscape (fig. 51); the other two prints, however, are again so strongly ideogrammatic that the associations are hard to grasp. And so it goes on. The 'Elégieéquation', opening with the words 'L'hibiscus qui n'est pas autre chose qu'un oeil éclaté', has two plant stalks almost symmetrically placed, with blossoms which are, in fact, bursting eyes. Many of the ideogrammatic illustrations are of an erotic character and to avoid tiresome repetitions we refer only to one other poem, 'Ton portrait', a very pessimistic meditation on mankind. Its core is probably to be found in the following lines:

> *ne parlons pas des hommes*
> *seulement tas de poussière qui montent*
> *et regardent le paysage*
> *comme énormes voûtes de champignons.*

Whether Picasso's vegetative human figure (fig. 55) corresponds to the theme of these lines we hesitate to decide.

Of all the books illustrated by Picasso, *Corps perdu* seems to us the most problematic. Who can tell whether later generations will regard it with enthusiasm, with disapproval or with ridicule? But such as it is, text and illustrations are a faithful reflection of the present state of our civilization: turning back to the most primitive forms, flinching from no experiment, at once subtle and childlike.

No less hard to understand than Césaire's poems is a book published in the following year, Tristan Tzara's *De Mémoire d'homme*, which the author calls a poem although a great part of it is in prose. The surrealist text appears to be a poetic discussion of the cardinal problems of the world: life, time, nature. The fact that nature is of some importance in the book may explain why Picasso's eight full-page lithographs (the book is a large quarto, 325×250 mm.) represent nothing but plants and insects. The lithographs are highly ornamental (fig. 51)[53] and the title print[54] is composed, like those for the book by Césaire, with a blank space for the text. But the realistic designs do not seem to strike the right note as accompaniment to the surrealist poetry and this lack of stylistic unity leaves us dissatisfied. If many of the truly Picassoesque ideograms in the book by Césaire look like picture puzzles defying solution, the spirit which informed them was in

49.   Frontispiece to Aimé Césaire, *Corps perdu*, 1950. Etching.
337 × 242 mm. *See page 79*

LONGITUDE

50.   Fly-title from Aimé Cesairé, *Corps perdu*, 1950. Etching.
323 × 233 mm. *See page 80*

51.   Illustration from Tristan Tzara, *De mémoire d'homme*, 1950.
Lithograph. 271 × 188 mm. Mourlot, Picasso lithographe, III, 46.
See page 80

SERUIREZ A CEUX QUI CRAIGNENT DE SE NOYER, SI CE N'EST
QUE LES POINTES DE VOS DOIGTS, DE VOS GENOUX, DE VOS
COUDES, & DE VOS FLANCS LEUR OSTENT L'ENUIE D'APPROCHER
DE VOUS; CAR AUEC CES ARMES VOUS POUUEZ POIGNARDER,
PERÇER, TUER, SI BON VOUS SEMBLE, VOS ENNEMIS. AUSSI FAUT
IL ADUOÜER, QUE DE TOUTE VOSTRE PERSONNE VN BON ARTI-
SAN EN TIREROIT DES AIGUILLES, DES CLOUX, DES ALESNES,
DES CUREDENS, DES POIGNARDS, DES CHEUILLES DE LUTH, DES
CHASSIS, DES LANTERNES, & PRESQUE AUTANT DE BESOIGNES
QU'ON FAICT DE L'INDIEN & FAMEUX ARBRE COCOS; MAIS LE
PLUS SÇAUANT ALCHIMISTE N'EN SÇAUROIT TIRER VNE GOUTE
D'EAU, POURCE QU'EN LA COMPOSITION DE VOSTRE PERSONNE
IL N'ENTRA QUE DU FEU, DE L'AIR, & DE LA TERRE; AUSSI N'Y
A T'IL GAND, BAS, NY SOULIER QUE VOS DOIGTS NE ROMPENT,
OU NE PERÇENT DU PREMIER IOUR. QUE SI VOUS ESTES A L'E-
GLISE, VOS GENOUX A TRAUERS LE PAUÉ VONT CASSER LES OS
DES TRÉPASSEZ, QU'ON PEUT REPUTER HEUREUX EN QUELQUE
FAÇON, PUISQUE ESTANS SANS AME, ILS NE PEUUENT PAS SEN-
TIR CES POIGNANTES BLESSURES. MAIS D'OU VIENT QU'ESTANT

52.   Two pages from Adrian de Monluc, *La Maigre*, 19

LA PLUS DANGEREUSE DE TOUTES LES FEMMES, & SI POINTUE
QUE VOUS PERÇEZ LES ARMES A L'ESPREUUE DU MOUSQUET;
D'OU VIENT, DIS-IE, QUE CEUX QUI PRENNENT GARDE A LA
POLICE, NE VOUS OBLIGENT PAS DE PORTER, AU LIEU D'VNE
ROBE DE SOYE, VNE GAINE DE FER? POURQUOY, PUISQUE VO-
STRE CORPS EST PLUS SCABREUX QU'VNE LANGOUSTE, & PLUS PI-
QUANT QU'VN CILICE, OU VNE HAIRE; POURQUOY N'ALLEZ VOUS
DANS LES MONASTERES EMBRASSER LES PAUURES PENITENS, QUI
NE TROUUENT PAS ASSEZ D'INUENTIONS DEDANS N'Y DEHORS
LE MONDE, POUR SE MACERER? VOS EMBRASSEMENS SERONT AU-
TANT DE MORTIFICATIONS POUR EUX, CAR SE IOINDRE A VOUS
EST PLUSTOST VN ACTE DE PENITENCE, QUE DE PECHÉ; & IE
M'ASSEURE QUE SI CELUY QUI SE IETTOIT NUD PARMY LES ESPI-
NES POUR CHASTIER LES REBELLES MOUUEMENS DE SA CHAIR,
EUT RENCONTRÉ VN CORPS SI PICQUANT QUE LE VOSTRE, SANS
DOUTE QU'IL AUROIT COURU APRES VOUS. LES PEAUX DES HE-
RISSONS & DES PORCS-ESPICS SONT PLUS DOUCES, LES RONCES
& LES ORTIES PLUS SUPPORTABLES, & DONT IL Y A MOINS DE
DANGER D'APROCHER. CET INNOCENT QUI PENSANT FOLASTRER

tching. 78 × 386 mm. *See page 83*

LA QUERELLE D'APELLES & DE PROTOGENES, CELUI QUI VOUS

EUT APPLIQUÉE ENTRE LEURS LIGNES, SANS DOUTE EN EUST EM-

PORTÉ LE PRIX. QUE DONC CES AUARES & SUBTILS LÆSINEURS,

QUI FONT PROFESSION DE PARTIR VN CHEUEU EN DEUX, FACENT

LE SEMBLABLE DE VOSTRE PERSONNE, IE LES EN DÉFIE; QUE

3

53.   Two pages from Adrian de Monluc, *La Maigre*, 1952.

S'ILS Y PEUUENT PARUENIR, I'ADUOUERAY QU'ILS MERITENT DE
MESNAGER LES THRESORS, & LES FINANCES DU ROY. SANS DOU-
TE VOUS ESTES CET INDIUIDU VAGUE, SI SOUUENT NOMMÉ PAR
LES LOGICIENS, QUI NE SE DIT DE PERSONNE. LES ENCHAI-
NEURS DE PUCES NE VOUS SÇAUROIENT ATTACHER DE LEURS

4

Etching. 255 × 386 mm. *See page 83*

54.   Cover to Adrian de Monluc, *La Maigre*, 1952. Etching.
338 × 173 mm. *See page 83*

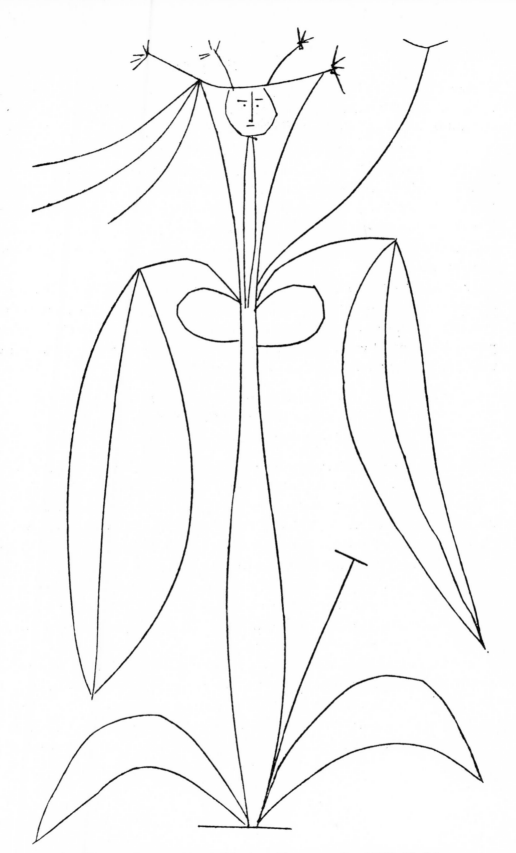

55.   Illustration to Aimé Césaire, *Corps perdu*, 1950. Etching.
334 × 203 mm. *See Page 80*

harmony with that of the poetry. In the book by Tzara we feel that the opposite is true. The only fundamental affinity which might be found lies in the decorative value of the prints: for Tzara, too, sheer melodiousness — the decorative element of poetry — is of such moment that it may be asked whether certain passages do not owe their final form solely to considerations of euphony.

Erik Satie's *Cahiers d'un mammifère*, published by P. Aelberts of Liège as No. 22 of the series *Brimborions*, is a slender booklet containing aphorisms and a brief essay on the delights of the table written by the composer, together with reproductions of three pen drawings by Picasso which have no connection with Satie's text.

Le Visage de la Paix, published in 1951 by the Cercle d'Art, is a suite of twenty-nine drawings, two of them in colour, paraphrasing the theme of the human face with a dove and all made on one day, December 5, 1950. To accompany them, Eluard wrote aphorisms on peace and love of peace, which betray their Communist tendency only in one passage:

> *C'était en mil neuf cent dix sept*
> *Et nous gardons l'intelligence*
> *De notre délivrance.*

The volume is not an illustrated book in the true sense, but is built up on the same principle as the *Histoire naturelle* with the texts of Buffon. The difference is that the publisher there cut up an existing text to fit the subjects chosen by the artist, whereas here the text was written specially to go with the drawings. For the frontispiece of the *édition de luxe* (150 copies on pure rag paper) Picasso made a lithograph[55] which has the same subject and is dated September 29, 1951. It is interesting to compare the variations on the same theme, stylized to a great extent in spite of the basically realistic forms. The linear pencil drawings are printed in offset, while the frontispiece of the *de luxe* edition was drawn on the limestone in the original lithographic technique.

La Maigre by Adrian de Monluc, a literary curiosity which Iliazd has rescued from oblivion, dates from 1630 and is a savage and spiteful satire upon an excessively thin woman who boasts of her beauty and virtue. Like all books produced by Iliazd, his edition of 1952 shows great ingenuity. It consists of 12 sheets of 41 × 46 cm., printed on one side and folded into four-page sections of

Introduction

41 × 23 cm. The printed pages face each other on every second opening, with blank double-spreads on the reverse. The first four-page section has, on the third page, the title with the serial number of each copy and the limitation notice (14 copies on Japanese and 60 on Chinese paper), the second section has a short introduction by the editor, sections 3–9 contain the text and the etchings. These printed openings alternate in their lay-out: one has the text in two columns, each 175 mm. wide, in the upper three quarters, and the etching (78 mm. high and 386 mm. wide — the width of both columns plus the back margins) running across the bottom quarter (fig. 52); the next has the etching in the upper three quarters (255 × 386 mm., fig. 53) and the text in the bottom quarter. The text is set in a thin sans-serif type, not only because it inveighs against a thin woman, but also because this typeface goes astonishingly well with the black-and-white pattern of the mostly linear etchings. The type was again set by Iliazd himself, and by adjusting the letter-spacing exactly to the shape of each character he has achieved complete optical balance. For all its slimness, the volume as a whole is most attractive in its graphic design.

Picasso's etchings fit the unusual proportions exactly and must therefore have been made expressly for this book. Some of them, especially the three large-size prints, represent the lean woman in various postures. The four narrow oblong etchings of knightly scenes serve as a satirical backcloth and correspond well with the almost medieval coarseness of the story. The last print is in the nature of a tail-vignette: on the left, three small nudes in a landscape, and on the right an over-lifesize bird on a branch. A ninth etching, on the parchment sheet used as cover, also alludes to medieval knighthood: the two rearing wolves and the irregular geometric design on the quartered field obviously ridicule the heraldry of those ages and the caricatured head at the base underlines the satirical effect (fig. 54).

Considered as a work of art, the book as a whole has undoubtedly high qualities. It is not, indeed, a literary masterpiece, but a jest with a satirical tinge, and those who incline to think that only the greatest works of world literature have a right to sumptuous presentation will find this volume unrewarding. But those who would concede that lighter fare of great curiosity is also a legitimate pursuit of bibliophiles will acknowledge *La Maigre* to be an amusing find, produced in good taste and with subtle feeling for the canons governing fine book design.

56.   Illustration from Maurice Toesca, *Six contes fantasques*, 1953.
326 × 246 mm. *See page 85*

And if the credit for planning the production is probably due to Iliazd alone, Picasso, by submitting readily to the requirements of the book as a whole, has evidently co-operated as a true book artist.

At the end of 1953 Flammarion published the *Six Contes fantasques* by Maurice Toesca to which Picasso contributed six dry-point etchings. The stories are: The Birth of the Butterflies (in early Chinese art), The Second-Hand (which kills the young man trying to arrest the progress of time), The Birth of a Princess (who extricates an American millionaire from embarrassment on a Chinese train), The Walking Tree (which takes revenge for the cutting down of the forest), The Encounter with the Bird (an imaginary bird), The Hellish Forest (which turns into an enchanted forest). Picasso's prints represent: an almost over-lifesize realistic profile beside a small, greatly stylized female figure[56] (fig. 56), a female nude at her toilet, a large woman's head in profile, a greatly stylized ideogram, an almost equally stylized double head, and finally another large realistic head in profile. The book is set in the text size of the beautiful Grandjean Roman ('Romain du Roi', 1694) and exquisitely printed by the Imprimerie Nationale in an edition of 225 copies, 25 on Japanese paper with a suite of the etchings, and 200 on deckle-edged paper. But although Toesca's stories abound in incidents which lend themselves to illustration, a comparison of the contents with the subjects of Picasso's prints shows that there is not the slightest connection between them. One is left with the feeling that Picasso might just as well have given the publisher any other six of his prints.

The same can be said of the next publication. In 1954 appeared the first edition of a newly discovered story by Diderot, entitled *Mystification ou Histoire des portraits*. In it Diderot tells how, with the assistance of a charlatan who poses as a Turkish doctor, he induced Mlle. Dornet to part with four portraits of her former lover, Prince Galitzine, at the latter's wish. The book has four reproductions of drawings in Indian ink — excellent portraits of the same model, all dated February 14, 1954, and numbered XV, IV, II and VI. It is not far-fetched to suppose that these drawings were four out of fifteen or more which the artist had made of the model on that day. Text and illustrations have nothing in common beyond the fact that there are four portraits of the same person. Yet it would have been quite easy to represent incidents from Diderot's story, if Picasso had had the slightest intention of doing so.

Picasso as a Book Artist

Les Cavaliers d'ombre, a volume of poems by Geneviève Laporte, came out in 1954. The publisher was J. Foret, who had not entered the bibliophile market previously, and who was glad, no doubt, to have for his first venture a book illustrated by Picasso. Although the volume went out of print very quickly and thus justified his confidence, its design is open to criticism.

A sumptuous folio of 41 × 33 cm., it contains fourteen poems written in 1951–1953. Every other poem is illustrated with a Picasso drawing etched on copper by Georges Bétemps and signed by Picasso on the plate. As far as we can see, there is no connection between the drawings and the poems. The first poem, which has given the book its title, describes a dream about a kind of apocalyptic horseman who tries to lay the sleeper under a spell; she resists the temptation and prefers the happiness of awaking peacefully in the arms of her lover. The corresponding illustration represents a sleeping girl. The third poem, 'Présage chanson', is a rhymed lament of a forsaken girl, framed by a kind of refrain which speaks of birds — ravens, blackbirds, eagles, wood-pigeons — dancing in the air and dying. This is accompanied by one of the famous drawings of owls, signed 'pour toi G. Vallauris 25 août 1951 Picasso'. (Whether the 'G' refers to the Christian name of the authoress we cannot say.) The fifth poem, 'Après l'amour', tells of a man drunk with love, who dances over the roof-tops until he falls headlong to the ground, where his broken body finds release. The female nude who pulls on a slipper on her left foot, far from being an illustration of the text, strikes us as particularly discordant. The seventh poem, 'Sillages', recalls an hour which two people spent together, when time seemed to them to stand still. The illustration is again at variance with the text: a tiny figure seated on clouds, a kind of miniature Zeus, hurling thunderbolts, with the sun beating down fiercely from above. The ninth poem, 'Scaphandre', is the lament of a woman who cannot escape from her love; the illustration: a crouching nude. (It may be mentioned that the poem is dated from July 19, 1951, and the drawing from August 25, 1951.) The next illustrated poem, 'Sur la mort de Midjuck' is an elegy in tragic strain on the death of the 'One'. That this 'One' is a dog is suggested by some lines (but only some) of the poem. The illustration is a fine drawing of a Scotch terrier. Finally 'A l'heure du midi': the hour of noon, 'où les démons s'éveillent', magically unites man and nature. This is illustrated by a seated female figure.

Introduction

However fine most of Picasso's drawings are, they are reproduced by a method which is open to criticism, and have in most cases no connection with the text. We are left with the impression that the book as a whole has not grown organically, but has been put together.

In 1954 appeared a publication which must not remain unnoticed although it can hardly be described as an illustrated book. It is a suite of 14 sheets of 50 × 65 cm., folded as 56 pages of 25 × 32 cm. The text occupies 26 pages, the other 30 pages contain drawings. The text opens with the date 12-2-41; it consists evidently of several independent pieces — Picasso calls them poems — apparently written at different times. The drawings are all dated from April and May, 1949, and have no connection with the text: there are birds, heads of men and women, a few landscapes, some compositions, a first version of the illustration to *Poésies des mots inconnus*, mentioned above. One would think that Picasso had some purpose in combining these texts and graphic works on the fourteen sheets, but the whole looks like an entirely haphazard collection, a kind of note-book which, like a sketch-book, comprises ideas that have nothing to do with one another. Similar books have been published occasionally by other artists; this publication can luckily be numbered among Picasso's graphic works.[57]

Tristan Tzara's poem *A haute flamme* was published in the spring of 1955, in an edition limited to seventy copies. The title-page contains the author's name, the title and, in addition, only the name Pablo Picasso. Any suggestion of illustration has been avoided and, in our opinion, rightly. This surrealist poem of about 500 lines (on 37 pages) is a melancholy evocation of memories of old times, typical of a man who finds, not without sorrow, that he has grown old. The five etchings by Picasso do not appear to have anything in common with each other or with the text, and vary even in size. A head, opposite the title, is 52 × 43 mm.; the second print, a female torso, 117 × 85 mm.; the third, a strongly stylized face, the left half oval and the right triangular, 74 × 60 mm.; the fourth, a deformed female nude, also very strongly stylized, 120 × 96 mm.; the last print, another head, also stylized, but not as much as the first, is also 74 × 60 mm. The only etching which was undoubtedly made for the book is that printed on the wrapper (size of the book 227 × 154 mm., size of the etching, 210 × 144 mm.). It is a dry-point with the words TZARA / A HAUTE FLAMME / PICASSO in capital letters. We find this wrapper not very successful. Where

Picasso uses his own handwriting, as in the *Gongora*, the result can be charming and effective. Here, instead of writing naturally, he tried his hand at 'calligraphy', and that is not his strong point. Neither the cuneiform character of the lettering nor its asymmetrical position seems to us quite satisfactory.

The first volume of 1956, Roch Grey's poem *Chevaux de minuit*, edited by Iliazd, is an unusual one and of special interest in many respects. Its history is itself extraordinary. The manuscript was completed in 1936 and the poet left it with Picasso, who was to illustrate it. Many eventful years passed, Grey died, and still no progress was made. After Picasso had discussed the publication with Iliazd, many more years were to pass until the latter, after long experiments in his composing room, found a typographical form that satisfied him, and at last the poem was published, twenty years after it had been written.[58]

Composed in free rhythms, it is a nostalgic evocation of former times, when the horse was man's faithful companion and his only means of fast transport (with the horse-power of engines leading up to an unexpected brief hymn in praise of aeroplanes). The underlying mood is well summed up in the introductory poem 'Devant une gravure ancienne':

> *Regrettez-vous le temps des ballades*
> *Des randonnées à cheval dans une nuit obscure*
> *Des fantasques pilleurs-cavaliers*
> *Des vierges campées dans un farouche donjon*
> *Au fond d'une sombre forêt. . . .*

The horse, which has disappeared from our roads together with the 'good old days', is celebrated by Grey in a style which, though not exactly traditional, is in no way surrealist or hermetic. Picasso contributed twelve dry-point etchings, which in spite of deliberate deformations make a strongly realistic impression and thus correspond in style with the text. They were made in close collaboration with the book designer, and their size and quality of line are perfectly adapted to the typography. All twelve prints have the same width of 15·5 cm.; the first and last are 23 cm. high and occupy the imaginary type area, while the ten which illustrate the text are 21 cm. high so as to leave room for a few lines of type underneath. Only the etching on the wrapper, a thirteenth print, is 17·5 × 21·5 cm. and differs slightly from the size of the book, not without good reason. In passing it may be mentioned that the first ten etchings in the book are dated '15–IV–55 Cannes' and the last two '27–IV–56'.

In other books which we have described it was Picasso who made the experiments, here it is the book designer, Iliazd. He has divided the book into seventeen units, of which some consist of four, others of three leaves. The units of four leaves contain only text: the first and last pages have been left blank and the text occupies the six inner pages. The units of three leaves are composed as triptychs: the verso pages are blank, of the recto pages that in the centre contains an etching with one or a few lines of text, the other two contain only text, which occupies no more than the lower third or quarter of the type area.[58a] This typographical design gives the book great charm and coherence. The units which contain only text are set with great ingenuity and impeccable taste, in the same sans-serif capitals which Iliazd had used for his Monluc edition. He again took pains to balance each word by individual letter-spacing until he was perfectly satisfied with the optical result. The infinite patience required to achieve this can be fully appreciated only by those who, like the present writer, have practical experience of the labour involved. The appearance of the book fully justifies the pains taken by the typographer. In one point, however, the production is not entirely satisfactory: the book falls apart, literally, into its component units. The flow of the poetry is interrupted unduly by the many blank pages, and if one has the book bound (which is after all the usual way of preserving a bibliophile publication) the 'triptychs' must be guarded — not an entirely satisfactory procedure.

We have already mentioned that the illustrations are as perfectly adapted to the typography as could be wished, but their treatment of the subject is rather surprising. While the poet idealizes the horse and sings a hymn in praise of the 'noble steed', Picasso's horses, or most of them, are far from noble and have the appearance of heavy Flemish draught-horses rather than of Arab thoroughbreds. The tenth etching, which shows a horse sitting on its hind legs like a well-trained dog, makes us wonder whether it is our lack of imagination that fails to associate this posture with the idea of a 'noble steed'. Notwithstanding this reservation, *Chevaux de minuit* remains one of the most interesting of the books which Picasso really illustrated, and the edition was so small — fifty-two copies on Japanese paper and sixteen on Chinese paper for those who collaborated in the production — that it will soon be scarce and sought after by collectors.

Eluard's *Un poème dans chaque livre* of 1956 contains twelve poems, each accompanied by a print from the hand of a different artist. The poem illustrated by Picasso was written in 1932 and is entitled *La Vie immédiate*:

> *Le sang coulant sur les dalles*
> *Me fait de sandales*
> *Sur une chaise au milieu de la rue*
> *J'observe les petites filles créoles*
> *Qui sortent de l'écoles en fumant la pipe*

The corresponding etching, which is as big as two pages, is an ideogram which we have been unable to decipher and which, as far as we can see, has nothing to do with the poem.

The last book illustrated by Picasso in 1956 was Max Jacob's *Chronique des temps héroïques*. It is a volume of memoirs, and the 'heroic times' are those of modern art, from about 1905 to 1920. The chronicle is written in the surrealist style and consists of fragments of recollections, garnished with puns, anecdotal, sometimes polemical, always unsystematic, skipping constantly from one subject to another. The style is characterized by the numerous parentheses which Jacob can never suppress.

This book, which does not really lend itself in the least to illustration, was illustrated by Picasso, who also lithographed the wrapper and the cover of the slip-case. Twenty-four of his drawings were engraved on wood by Aubert (who had also collaborated on the Balzac) and are used as head- and tail-pieces to the eight main chapters and the numerous subdivisions. Three full-page etchings were made specially for the book: they are exactly the same size as the type area and are all dated 7.9.56.[58b] The frontispiece lithograph is dated Vallauris 23.9.53, and has the exact size of the book apart from a very narrow margin. The inscription at the top, 'Max Jacob', serves as complement to the title-page opposite, which has only the title, the name of the illustrator and that of the publisher. The heading shows that this lithograph is a portrait of the author. Two of the three etchings are also portraits of Max Jacob, the third is a half-length male nude seen from the back.

The twenty-four drawings are placed, as we have mentioned, at the beginning and at the end of the chapters. The eleven figure drawings at the heads of the chapters are reminiscent of the drawings to Balzac's *Le Chef-d'œuvre inconnu* and seem to have been made before 1930, which would make them almost contemporary with the period treated in the text. The twelve tail-pieces are mostly ornamental and may have been made specially for the book, as well as one full-page ornament. The cover of the slip-case is an 'illumination' as understood by Picasso: on the front a large spot made up of red lines, surrounded by eight black dots, on the back a spot made up of black lines, surrounded by six red dots. The book jacket is in 'calligraphy': on top the name of the author, at the bottom the title (both in black), in the middle an elongated red field made up of broad stripes. Fortunately Picasso has here refrained from using anything but his natural handwriting and consequently the result is much more organic than his lettering for Tristan Tzara's *A haute flamme*.

It is easy to understand why Picasso contributed the illustrations to this book. He was a good friend of Jacob's until the latter's premature death in 1944, and Jacob describes Picasso's own 'heroic age', devoting many pages to him and to their common friend Apollinaire. A few of the best-known names mentioned in the book will be sufficient to explain Picasso's interest: Gertrude Stein, Raynal, Salmon, Chevrier, Reverdy, Tzara, Roch Grey, Kahnweiler, Braque, Cendrars, Cocteau. But he did not take a great deal of trouble. His illustrations are visual decorations, which admittedly go well with the book: his drawings conjure up the stylistic period treated in the text, his full-page prints portray his friend, the author. The wrapper and the cover of the slip-case, on the other hand, are true works of book decoration. But however convincing the general lay-out, the volume does not show Picasso's work for books at its best.

A passage on page 95 of the *Chroniques* explains why Picasso has a closer relation to book illustration than many other painters. Jacob tells us that Picasso had sought the ideal of perfection in drawing, which had been the aim of his life, and he goes on to quote the artist's own words: 'I don't know whether I am a great painter, but I am a great draughtsman.'[59] And that is one of the essential qualities of the great illustrator: he must be a great draughtsman. Those who find their true fulfilment in painting, who regard drawings only as preliminary studies and graphic prints only as by-products, may achieve eminence in the realm of art, but never in the field of book illustration.

Picasso as a Book Artist

The most recent book fully illustrated by Picasso was produced, once again, by Iliazd, and it may be said at once that it seems to us the most successful of all those on which the two men collaborated: *Le Frère Mendiant o Libro del conocimiento*, published in 1959. This is an early Spanish description of an African journey, for a long time known only in a shortened French version, until the Spanish original was rediscovered. Iliazd has edited the text in both languages from the old manuscripts in the British Museum and in the Biblioteca Nacional in Madrid, and the Spanish version in particular has gained a great deal from his revision. The text is set again in a sans-serif typeface, each word being spaced individually as required, in accordance with aesthetic principles of typography (the impressum refers to 'caracteres de espacio variable'); but a comparison with Iliazd's earlier publications shows that he has now attained to greater simplicity of book design. Pages of unequal sizes, such as he had used in *Pis'mo*, and other eccentricities, however ingenious, are never as satisfying in the long run as the classic calm of the traditional book page.

The book was printed in an edition of 54 copies on Japanese paper and consists of 24 sheets of 41 × 62 cm., printed on one side only and folded once, each page measuring 41 × 31 cm. The type area is divided into two columns of about 31 × 12·5 cm. The size of the etchings is based on that of the type area: the half-page etchings have the size of a single column, the double-page etchings correspond to the two type areas of an opening including the back margins. Each of these double-page etchings is composed of two independent halves, which correspond to the facing pages of a normal text opening.

The twenty-four openings are arranged as follows: (1) complete title and *justification du tirage*, occupying the whole first column of the right-hand page; (2) preface by Iliazd, the French text in the two columns on the left and the Spanish translation on the right; (3) fly-title to the French text (one column only, as on the first opening); (4) beginning of the French text; (5) double-spread etching, on the left the head of a bull, on the right a fanciful coat of arms made up of elements taken from Spanish city emblems; (6) end of the French text; (7) fly-title to the Spanish text (one column as on the first opening). Sheets 8, 10, 12, 14, 16, 18, 20 and 22 contain the Spanish text, set in three columns of each opening, while the first column of each left-hand page contains an etching. These eight etchings represent standard-bearers holding the blazons

92

E PARTIMOS DE LA INSOLA DE GROPIS Ɛ
TOMAMOS CAMINO CONTRA EL LEUANTE
POR EL MAR MEREDIANO Ɛ FALLAMOS
OTRA ISLA QUE DIZEN QUIBLE ESTA ISLA
QUYBLE ES YA EN EL MAR MEREDIONAL
Ɛ ES POBLADA DE GENTES NEGROS Ɛ
DEXAMOS LA A MAN DERECHA Ɛ TOMAMOS
APRES DE LA RIBERA Ɛ PARESÇIO VN
MONTE MUY ALTO QUE DEZIAN ABBOCH Ɛ
FUEMOS ALLA Ɛ ERA TODO POBLADO DE
MUCHAS GENTES Ɛ NASÇIA DEL VN RIO
MUY GRANDE Ɛ ERA TIERA MUY ABONDADA
Ɛ DE AQUY SE TORNO LA GALEA Ɛ YO
FINQUE ALLI VN TIENPO Ɛ DESPUES PARTY
DE ALBOCH CON GENTES Ɛ FUY A OTRO
MONTE QUE DIZEN LIRRY Ɛ NASÇIA DEL
VN RIO QUE DIZEN ENALCO Ɛ PARTI
DESTE MONTE QUE DIZEN LIRRI Ɛ FUY
AL REYNADO DE GOTONIE QUE TIENE MUY
GRANDES TIERAS POBLADAS Ɛ YERMAS Ɛ
EN ESTE REYNADO GOTONIE SON VNOS
MONTES MUCHO ALTOS QUE DIZ QUE NON
SON OTROS TAN ALTOS EN EL MUNDO
Ɛ DIZENLES LOS MONTES DE LA LUNA
OTROS LES DIZEN LOS MONTES DEL ORO
E NASÇEN DESTOS MONTES ÇINCO RIOS
LOS MAYORES DEL MUNDO Ɛ VAN TODOS
CAER EN EL RIO DEL ORO Ɛ FAZE Y VN
LAGO TAN GRANDE DE VEYNTE JORNADAS
EN LUENGO Ɛ DIEZ EN ANCHO Ɛ FAZE
EN MEDIO VNA GRAND ISLA QUE DIZEN
PALOLA Ɛ ES POBLADA DE GENTES
NEGROS PERO LA MAS DESTA TIERRA
ES DESABITADA POR LA MUY GRAND
CALENTURA Ɛ POR QUE
ES TODA ARENAS
MUERTAS

57.   A page from *Le Frère Mendiant o Libro del conocimiento*, 1959.
Page size 410 × 310 mm. *See pages 92–93*

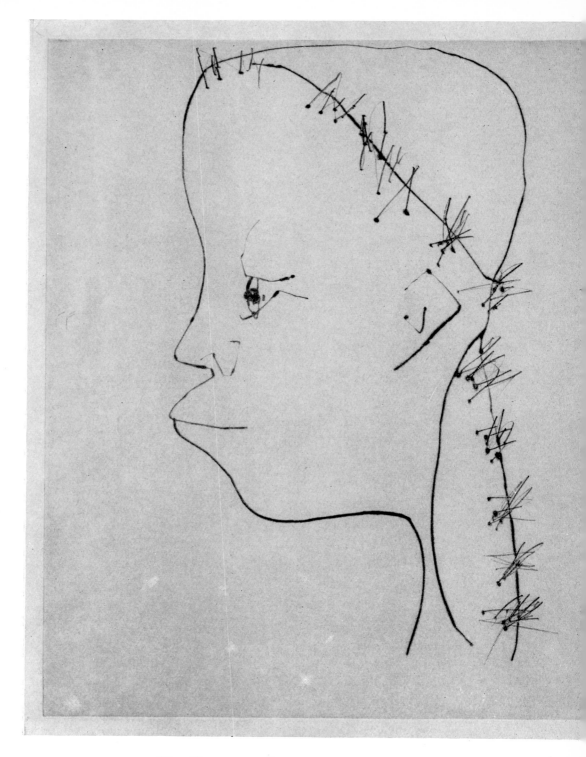

58.   Two pages from *Le Frère Mendiant o Libro del conocimie*

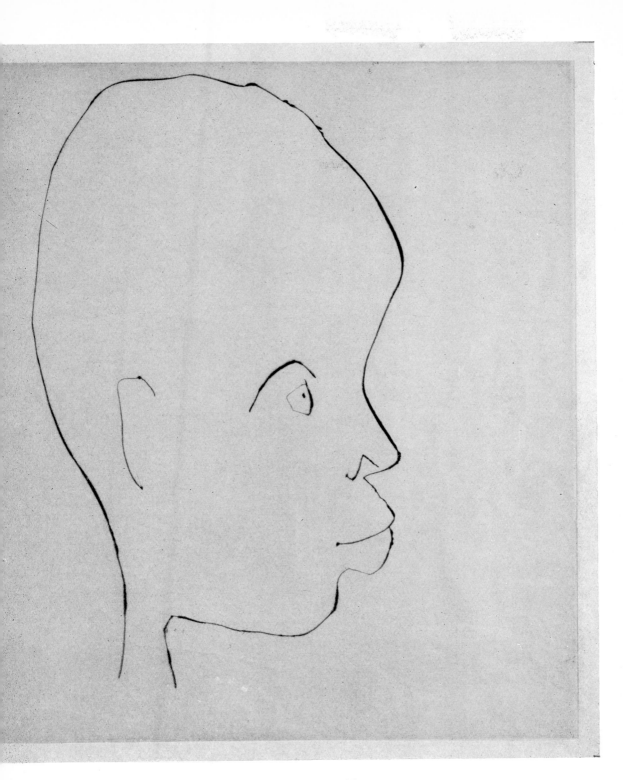

1959. Size of double spread 410 × 620 mm. *See page 93*

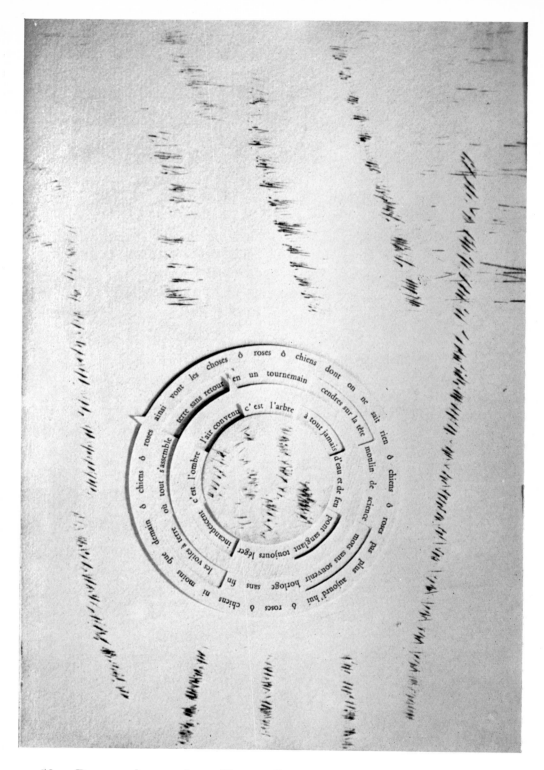

59.   Decorated page from Tzara: *La rose et le chien*, 1958. Etching of revolving wheel. *See pages 96–98. Photo: Pablo Volta*. 260 × 165 mm.

of the provinces described on the same opening. Picasso has based the emblems on the heraldic representations decorating one of the medieval manuscripts of the Spanish text (see fig. 57). The double-spread etchings between the eight sheets just mentioned have African themes and are entitled as follows: (9) *El Desierto* (The Desert): on the left an African house, on the right an oasis; (11) *Los hombres* (The Men): two Negro heads; (13) *El velero* (The Sailing-Ship): on the left the ship, on the right a landscape; (15) *Las mujeres* (The Women): two female torsos; (17) *Rio Abajo*: on the left a river landscape with a boat and mountains in the background, on the right a native house on piles; (19) *Los niños* (The Children): on the left the head of a Negro girl, on the right the head of a Negro boy (fig. 58); (21) *Las flores* (The Flowers): one flower on the left and another on the right. Sheet 23 carries an editorial notice ('Fuentes del texto'), and the last, No. 24, contains a list of the sheets for the guidance of the bookbinder, and the colophon.

Like previous publications of Iliazd, the book has a parchment cover. This is decorated with the same etching as the fifth opening, the right half of which appears on the front of the cover and the left half on the back. In this way heraldic arms of Spanish character serve to announce the contents of the book, a point which derives particular significance from the fact that the text had long given rise to arguments whether the French or the Spaniards had had priority in the modern exploration of Africa — a dispute which only the discovery of the original Spanish manuscript of the *Libro del conocimiento* resolved in favour of Spain. The linear, naturalistic bull's head on the back of the cover forms an effective tail vignette. Here, too, as in Iliazd's *Pis'mo*, one must admire the superb result achieved in the extremely difficult process of printing an etched plate on parchment.

Our description of the illustrations will have made it clear that they are not incidental decorations, but were designed and etched for this particular text and indeed for the particular edition planned by Iliazd. The design of the book as a whole is successful in every respect, except, perhaps for the fact that the printing on single sheets makes the binding a problem and renders it necessary to place the sheets on guards, a procedure which is not entirely satisfactory either from the technical or from the aesthetic point of view and which leads to the further disadvantage that, when the pages are turned, every printed opening is followed by a blank opening. The latter drawback could have been avoided, in theory, if paper of double size had been used and four pages had been printed on the outside of each sheet, the first page containing two text columns, the second and third a double-spread etching, and the fourth a standard-bearer and one column of text. The sheets could then have been folded in concertina fashion, and the whole been bound as a block-book. This method, however, would have presented other difficulties: Japanese paper is not available in size 41 × 124 cm., the printing of such a long strip is not advisable, and when bound, the paper might have cockled, a risk which every book-designer wishes to avoid.

We must now go back a few years to describe a dozen slim booklets which we think are best considered as a homogeneous group. They were published from 1956 to 1960 by the printer, poet and amateur publisher P. A. Benoit in the village of Alès (Département Gard) in Southern France. Benoit had previously published small booklets in limited editions — small both in size and in bulk, though most of them probably still much too big for collectors of miniature books. Nine of the twelve publications mentioned contain only one print by Picasso and would, in a formalistic classification, be reckoned among those for which the artist merely made a frontispiece. We prefer nevertheless to group them with the illustrated books because we consider that a poem of a dozen short, in some cases extremely short, stanzas finds a full visual equivalent in a single print, and that an over-rigid scheme, which merely counts without regard to the true relationship between text and illustration, does not do justice to their real significance. If Benoit had published the twelve poems with their etchings not singly, but in one volume, they would still have made a slim booklet, but one that would have been generally regarded as fully illustrated. In our bibliography we therefore list them not among the books decorated with a frontispiece, but among those illustrated by Picasso.

The first of the twelve publications was *Nuit* by René Crevel, a poem of thirty-five lines, which had previously appeared in a periodical and was reprinted by Benoit in a booklet of 90 × 65 mm. The etching which Picasso made specially for this edition is only 29 × 49 mm., a most unusual size for the artist. It represents a face, formed by three broken lines for eye-brows and mouth, two small circles for the eyes, and an acute angle with two dots for the nose, framed in an upright rectangle. Whether Picasso had read the poem we cannot

B.   Cover of the catalogue: *Picasso, Les Ménines*, 1959.
Lithograph.

say; he certainly made not the slightest attempt to capture its spirit, which can be summed up in one phrase: oppressive nocturnal sleeplessness. His etching would have been equally suitable or unsuitable for any other poem which expresses human thoughts.[60]

The same applies to the next publication, the poem *Autre chose*, in which Benoit expresses man's striving after ever new sensations and experiences. Picasso's etching — a view of the sunlit sky over the sea — has no apparent relevance to the text. But the relation between text and illustration was soon to undergo a radical change.

The third publication, another poem by Benoit, entitled *Picasso derrière le masque*, appeared at the beginning of 1957. As the poem has Picasso himself for its theme, we quote it in full, by kind permission of the author:

PICASSO DERRIÈRE LE MASQUE

Le pied
touche la terre
la main
une autre main

les yeux regardent
ce que nous voyons
et voient
bien au delà

la parole
court
mais écoute
une autre voix

le geste cache
et révèle

ce qui se passe
devant
malmène
ce qui se passe
derrière

l'eau de la source
se colore
de sang
martyrisée
pour qu'elle
crie

le souffle
est au-dessus
appelé
par le vide

95

la tête seule

est caressée

la tête

qui fait

tout manœuvrer

la tête

qui sait

le masque

paroi protectrice

permet

le repli

dans les secrets

qui se laissent

percer

plus à l'aise

il permet

de fixer

pour fouiller

les lointains

si proches

mais

permet

aussi de réserver

le feu

qui fuse

de l'iris

point

que rien

n'obstrue

la porte

par où passer

pour brûler

sur soi

ce qui retient

d'abord

The etching which Picasso contributed represents a mask, and the slight irony which may be discerned in it suggests that the artist may have thought of his own face.

After an interval of fourteen months, in March 1958, Benoit published Tristan Tzara's *La rose et le chien*. This literary and typographical curiosity is a poem of three stanzas, the lines of which can be interchanged in several combinations. To make this possible, some of the lines have been printed on a wheel which can be rotated to obtain different permutations. This device is no novelty in books, for similar wheels had been used already in some astronomical works of the sixteenth century, but here we have the only instance known to us of its use in modern book production. The entire design of the book was in the hands of Picasso, who contributed an etched frontispiece, planned the lay-out of the

tristan tzara

pablo picasso

p a b

60. Title page to Tzara, *La rose et le chien*, 1958. *See pages 96–98.*
Photo: *Pablo Volta.* 260 × 165 mm.

title-page, made a purely ornamental etching for the revolving wheel (see figs. 59-61) and etched a circular tail vignette for the page containing the colophon. As a second curiosity within the first, it is worth recording that below the wheel, and thus hidden from the reader, the printer has set a curse upon anyone who destroys the book by removing the wheel.

The next two publications appeared only two months later, in May 1958. Benoit's poem *Pierres* has a symbolic-ethical theme. Human relations, it asserts, may be likened to a heap of stones supporting one another: if men support each other, they can master the impossible. The poem ends with the lines:

> *Si nous nous rencontrons*
> *nez à nez*
> *ce n'est*
> *pas sans raison*
> *ne fuis pas*
> *une chance*
> *nous est*
> *donnée*

This has been illustrated by Picasso in a witty and successful etching: a double face which, nose against nose, looks into its own eye (fig. 63).

René Char's *L'escalier de Flore* is a pamphlet in large quarto, almost folio size: 350 × 235 mm., consisting of six leaves, of which three contain type (title, a prose poem of two paragraphs, and the colophon) and one a full-page etching in two colours. The text is an exclamation upon the fate of the poet, and the print, which Picasso made specially for it, represents a highly stylized human figure with a hypertrophic head: the poet himself.[60a] Below the unpretentious colophon there is a strange tail vignette of irregular and bizarre shape etched by Picasso. He also made an unusual cover design: three red vertical strokes arranged irregularly, three irregular oblique-horizontal strokes above an irregular cut-out trapezium. The strokes are not printed, but are formed by silk cords.

The poem *Si large mon image*, dated from the last day of the same year, is a particular curiosity in so far as only two copies were printed, one for Benoit, the author, and the other for Picasso, the illustrator. It consists of sixteen short lines set in a very large size of type, each page — oblong, 120 × 255 mm. — containing only two lines. The poem is an *aperçu* on the contradiction between the range of man's perceptions and the limitation of his capabilities. An abstract thought of this nature does not of course permit of illustration in the proper sense. Picasso's etching, an irregular pentagon 55 mm. high and 180 mm. wide, which reduces the human face to its essentials by means of two arched projecting lines (eye-brows), two dots (nostrils), a short horizontal (mouth), and two small unequal circles in white (pupils), seems to us a very suitable graphic counterpart to the text.

No publication of Benoit's appeared in 1959, but in 1960 five were published at short intervals, three of which contain poems by Benoit. The first, published in March and entitled *Meurs*, describes the death of a bull in the corrida and was then the smallest book printed by Benoit and illustrated by Picasso so far (a still smaller book was to appear in June, see below). Its size, 33 mm. high and 45 mm. wide, will satisfy even those collectors of miniature books who are most exacting in their demands. The frontispiece represents a dying bull, and since it bleeds off the page, Picasso has written his signature on the right half of the same leaf at the end of the text so that it appears on the right half of the same four-page section which has the frontispiece on its left half (fig. 64).

In April appeared the second poem by Benoit, *Vers où l'on voit*, in praise of the Provençal landscape. It is printed in normal octavo size and contains a landscape etching by Picasso.

The booklet *Température*, dated June 1960 and printed in a size of 21 × 40 mm., is devoted to an aphorism by Jacqueline Roque: 'Why are our hearts so easily chilled? No sooner do we open them than the slightest draught makes us shut them again.' Benoit has distributed this text over four pages, adding two preliminary leaves and two leaves for the colophon. Picasso contributed four etchings: on the front of the cover, a sailing-boat on the water; in the text, one of a landscape with radiant sun and another of grasses and a tree swaying in the breeze; and on the back of the cover, a landscape of dunes. All four prints have exactly the same size as the page and thus the margins of the copper-plates do not appear in the book and there is no room for the artist's signature. This is the smallest of all books containing a Picasso print.

René Char's *Pourquoi la journée vole*, published in July 1960, is likewise no more than an aphorism, though slightly longer, and deals with the poet's relationship to his surroundings. Picasso's etching, a greatly stylized recumbent female nude, appears to have no connection with the text, and the same applies to the stylized standing female nude which forms the frontispiece to Benoit's poem *Toute la vie*, published in August 1960.

This completes our analysis of Picasso's work as illustrator in so far as it has been disseminated by the printing press. A few words remain to be said about his work of decoration and illustration devoted to single copies of books and not intended for reproduction.

One such example became more widely known in 1959 with the publication, under the title *40 dessins en marge du Buffon*, of forty drawings which Picasso had made for the copy of Buffon's *Histoire naturelle* owned by Dora Maar. This must have been an easy task for him as, having illustrated Buffon's text once before, he had no new problems to solve. Besides, any animal drawing can serve as appropriate illustration to a work such as Buffon's. How much Picasso delights in decorating books is shown more clearly by other examples.

Fig. 62 shows a title-page on which Picasso has inscribed a dedication as a calligraphic ornament, fig. 65 the front cover of the leather-bound manuscript of 'Docteur Faustroll' by Jarry with a drawing made for it by Picasso and branded into the light brown skin. Both volumes are owned by the poet Tristan Tzara.

In his catalogue 'Poésie contemporaine; Picasso et l'art d'aujourd'hui' (published in 1957, but not dated), the Paris bookseller Jean Hugues describes under No. 358 a copy of the Picasso monograph by Jean Cassou (Paris, Editions Hypérion, 1940), containing not only annotations by Picasso on the paintings reproduced, but also numerous crayon drawings by him. Two of these are illustrated on the front and the back of the catalogue. As we have not inspected the book, it seems best to translate here the bookseller's description:

'Unique copy of the Picasso album by J. Cassou, revised, illustrated and embellished by the artist for Eluard.

'In 1943, when Picasso had doubtless more leisure than usual, he turned it to account by filling one copy of this art book with a work whose value, both documentary and artistic, is truly extraordinary. It is in fact under both aspects — as a document and as a work of art — that we have to regard the creation of what must be called an unpublished work of Picasso himself.

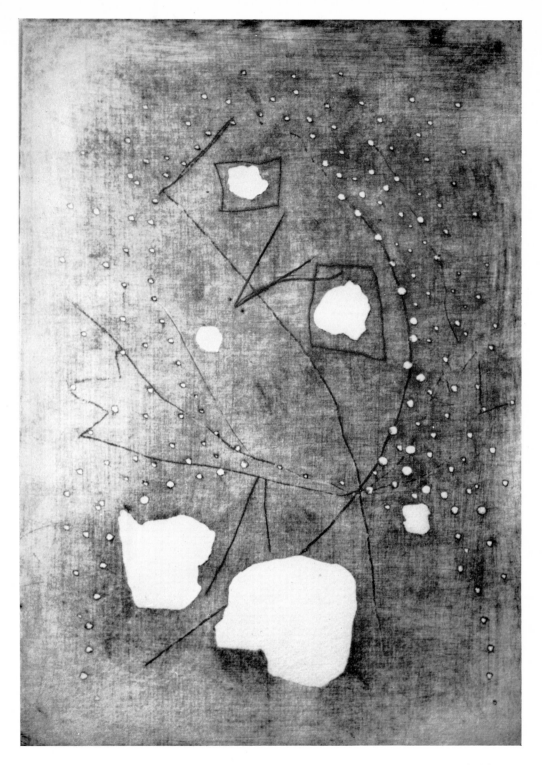

61. Frontispiece to Tzara, *La rose et le chien*, 1958. *See pages 96–98.*
Photo: Pablo Volta. 260 × 165 mm.

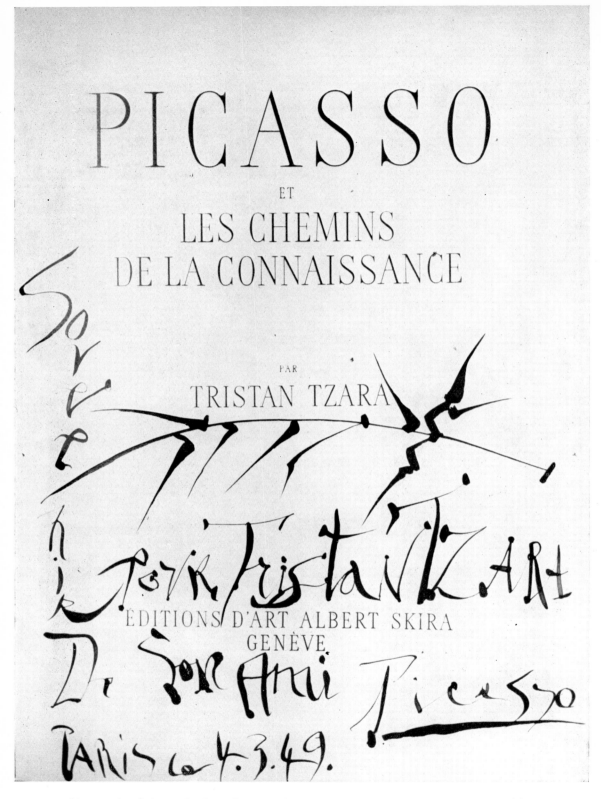

62.   A book inscribed by Picasso for Tzara. 400 × 310 mm. *See page 98.*
Photo: Pablo Volta.

64. Illustration to P. A. Benoit: *Meurs*, 1960. Etching. Original size. *See page 99*

63. Illustration to P. A. Benoit: *Pierres*, 1958. Etching. Original size. *See page 98*

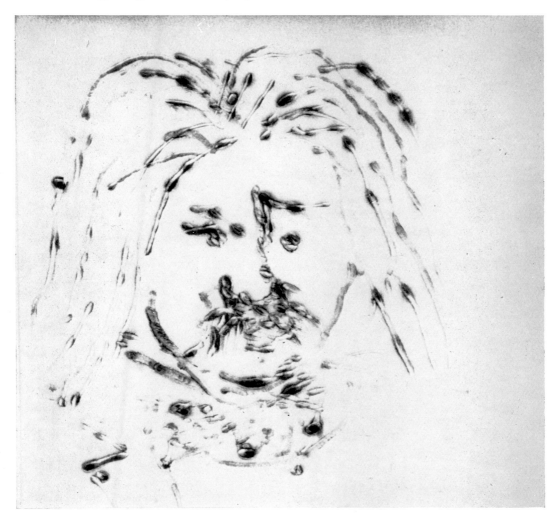

65. Front cover of leather-bound manuscript of *Docteur Faustroll* by Jarry branded with a design by Picasso. 200 × 170 mm. *See page 98*. *Photo: Pablo Volta.*

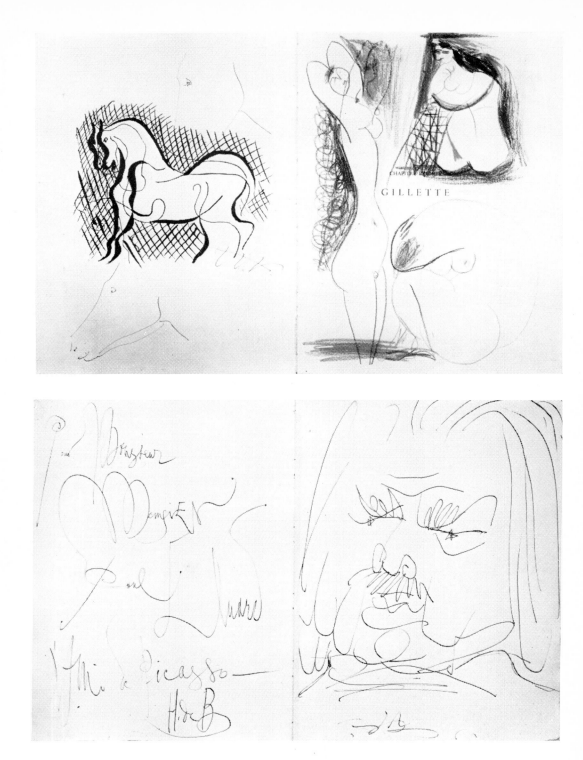

66. Two double spreads from *Picasso revu par Picasso*, 1943.
Crayon drawings. *See pages 100–101*

Introduction

'In the first place the artist has corrected or amplified all the explanatory captions printed below the monochrome and colour reproductions of his pictures. [Here follows a description of the additions and corrections made by Picasso.]

'This original revision would alone give the book an exceptional interest. But perhaps even more exciting are the ornamentation and illustration in which this amazing artist indulged freely in the margins and even on the actual reproductions. Using coloured crayons of vivid tints, he has filled the white and spotless pages with magnificent compositions in colour, among them the admirable cockerel and the vase of flowers reproduced on the cover of our catalogue. In addition he has framed the text and the reproductions on each page with many-coloured ornaments, adapting their hues and arabesques, with marvellous sureness and versatility, to the style and period of the works reproduced. Finally — and this is perhaps the triumph of Picasso's particular genius, carried away by an unceasing urge to explore, by an ever imperious need of invention and renewal — he has covered the reproductions with lines and colours which transform rather than correct or amplify them, and has thus literally re-composed some of his works in an unexpected return, as it were, of the creative fever that had inspired the original composition. We have here a singular parallel to a painter's retouching and reworking of pictures he painted earlier, but with this difference that Picasso, supremely indifferent to the materials he deals with, has no hesitation in using the modest reproductions of this album as a basis and pretext. With astonishment one follows, page after page, the painter's masterly pictorial commentary on his own work; a commentary which has doubtless no precedent in the work of other artists, and yet how thrilling would be a collection, in some ideal museum, consisting of a series of similar "artist's self-portraits".

'This precious copy belonged to Paul Eluard, who called it "Picasso revu par Picasso", a title inscribed on the spine of the binding, which was made for him by Saulnier'. [Here follow a few details of handwritten additions made by Eluard.]

These few examples, which have come to our knowledge, show how a book as such inspires Picasso to ornament and illustrate. It is quite possible that other and no less interesting examples have remained unknown in private hands.

Picasso as a Book Artist

OUR REVIEW of that portion of Picasso's graphic work which is to be found in books will enable us to draw twofold conclusions: first, concerning its place in the artist's oeuvre as a whole and, secondly, concerning the development of modern book illustration and the impact which Picasso's contribution made on it.

Picasso's graphic work in books — not counting those with a frontispiece — is spread over fifty-one works, a not inconsiderable number for an artist in whose oeuvre it occupies only a very small place. Of these fifty-one works, no fewer than twenty-two contain prints that interpret the text in visual form, while two others contain 'illuminations', a type of book decoration that does not fall under the heading of illustration. Now we can also perceive to what extent the connoisseur quoted at the beginning of this study was justified in denying that Picasso had any illustrative ability. It is interesting to note that this opinion is shared by Sabartés, who states[61] quite plainly: 'Picasso dislikes to be fettered by commissions. It is notorious how little he cares to paint portraits to order or to illustrate books. Many books indeed have illustrations from his hand, but this is explained by the wealth of his output, which always allows him to find something more or less suitable if the customer is not too fastidious. And his works are so valuable, and lend such prestige to the books in which they appear, that only few people raise objections if such contributions have not been specially made to order.'

These words apply in fact to more than half the books 'illustrated' by Picasso. They are true of *Le Siège de Jérusalem*, which appeared when he was thirty years old, of *Le Chef-d'œuvre inconnu*, when he was fifty, of Iliazd's *Afat*, when he was sixty, and of *Carmen*, which appeared when he was almost seventy. Picasso is deeply loyal to his friends, and his connections with many writers date partly from the days of his youth. That is why he has so often complied with requests for graphic contributions even when a text interested him much less than the author or the editor. As a result, some of the books we have described contain prints which delight by their beauty, but have little relevance to the text, the most impressive being probably those in the *Histoire naturelle*.

But this must not make us lose sight of the other twenty-four titles, which make up no less than 47 per cent of Picasso's work for books, and which the friend we have quoted and Sabartés appear to have ignored. The *Métamorphoses* and the *Lysistrata* are certainly illustrated books in the strictest sense of the term, for the tales by Reventós he has re-created in visual form the situations described by the author, and if we remember that he wrote out the Gongora sonnets with his own hand and added his own marginal drawings, and that he illuminated the manuscripts of contemporary poets such as Eluard and Reverdy, then we shall realize beyond doubt that attempts to reduce the work of this versatile artist to a single formula are apt to result in fallacies. To understand the range of Picasso's achievement as a book artist we must try to relate it to his own many-sidedness.

And his many-sidedness is not accidental. It is a characteristic of that group of modern artists of which Picasso is regarded as the prominent representative that they allow no preconceived ideas to govern their creative work, and this unhampered latitude in conception and in choice of technique explains why Picasso's work in the field of book design is a microcosm, an epitome, of the entire development of the illustrated book as sketched briefly in our introductory pages.

We meet the simplest form of book decoration in his 'illuminations' to Eluard's *Divers poèmes* and Reverdy's *Le Chant des morts*; initials in both editions of Reventós's tales, decorated chapter-headings and tail-pieces in *Carmen*, calligraphy with marginal drawings in *Gongora*, figure compositions of the traditional kind in Ovid, Aristophanes and Reventós. This variety of technique is matched by the diversity of conception. In Jacob's *Saint Matorel*, the cubist stylization allows the subject to function as correlate to the text, while a visual rendering of situations from the poem is deliberately avoided. At the opposite pole we have the Ovid, Aristophanes and Reventós, and an intermediate solution in the artist's own *Le Désir attrapé par la queue*, which is illustrated with a kind of stage designs. Finally we have the many books in which the first available prints were inserted solely to make up a precious collector's piece — they correspond to the sumptuous medieval manuscripts, which served in the first place to heighten the prestige of great lords. And if some of Picasso's attempts in the field of applied graphic art seem to us unsuccessful, his two designs for watermarks prove that his creative interest in craftsmanship extends also to book production.

All these aspects are united in the complex personality of this artist of genius. Jean Cassou once spoke of 'Picasso, who changes unceasingly and yet remains himself, who embraces all forms and all worlds. . . . There have been . . . strange geometries, daring deformations, metamorphoses, machines and theatrical illusions, a marvellous extension of the repertory of the spirit, explorations of everything, every play of a divinely creative imagination.'[62] These words, which refer to Picasso's art in general, can be applied without reservation to his graphic work in books. Only if this is borne in mind the great charm of his book decorations as a whole becomes fully apparent. We have pointed out at the beginning of this study why a systematic collection of Picasso's books will be beyond the reach of most. The few who succeed in assembling all the volumes on their shelves will undoubtedly have a source of infinite enjoyment.

What then is the significance of Picasso's work for modern book decoration? His most important achievement seems to us to be the introduction of cubism into the world of books. This was the prelude to all subsequent experiments of modern artists in the field of illustration. In what way these experiments will influence the general development of book decoration in the long run must be left to the judgement of later generations. There is still a lack of specialized research which would enable us to demonstrate the connections with the tendencies prevailing in the development of present-day book design. We must limit ourselves therefore to a few brief hints to clarify what we mean.

A comparison of modern illustrated books in daily use with those of former times shows at a glance the fundamental differences in approach. Children's books have taken on an entirely new look and the development of their artistic design has undergone greater changes during the last thirty years than in the entire previous century. It is beyond the scope of this study to prove that this development is closely linked with the tendencies of modern art, but one significant phenomenon may be pointed out: in the 1920's, when modern art was still influential in Russia, the native country of such distinguished artists as Kandinsky, Lissitzky, Malewitsch, Chagall, and others, Russian children's books stood in the forefront of this development. Later on, when every artistic movement aiming beyond 'socialist realism' was proscribed, the artistic quality of Russian children's books dropped rapidly and for the past twenty-five years they have lacked every significance.

In the field of documentary illustration a similar development has taken place, as every leading journal of the printing industry in Western Europe and the United States shows conclusively. Whether one thinks of the bleeding half-tone illustrations in the earliest years of modern typography (compare Picasso's etchings to *Dos Contes* by Reventós), of unorthodox placing of pictures in the type area, or of ultimate simplification in the artist's handling of the line — in each case we can find parallel tendencies in Picasso's prints.

We do not suggest that all these innovations in the design of illustrated books are due to Picasso, and we are even doubtful whether he has ever taken the trouble to reflect on such problems. That does not alter the fact that his *Saint Matorel* of 1911 represents the first encounter between modern art and the printed book. It dates from the time when the revival of European and American book design under the influence of William Morris was just beginning to carry the day. It was a revival born of retrospection and led to an enormous advance in the quality of books. But this advance extended to the material rather than to the artistic aspect, for it sprang from that return to good craftsmanship which put a stop to the unthinking routine prevailing in the printing industry of the late nineteenth century. These developments, however, broke no new ground and that is just what *Saint Matorel* did do. When Picasso made his four etchings for Jacob's book, he certainly did not suspect the consequences which his breach of seemingly well-established norms would have for future book illustration. It is a phenomenon that can be observed in all spheres of intellectual activity: the originally limited achievement of a man of genius giving rise to a development which he has not foreseen.

Bibliophiles, whose foremost concern is the book, will not value all publications illustrated by Picasso as highly as connoisseurs of the graphic arts, who enjoy a fine etching or a fine lithograph for its own sake, regardless of its relation to the surroundings in which it is placed. But even the bibliophile of strict principles will acknowledge some of Picasso's books to be among the finest illustrated books produced in our generation.

Notes

1. One example of such exceptions are the mushroom books. Mushrooms are such unaccountable and — it is tempting to exaggerate — unpredictable plants that they can be characterized more reliably by the brush of a sensitive artist than by the camera, which sees only one mushroom at a time, but is unable to render all the characteristics of the species because they are hardly ever combined in one specimen.

2. In his book *Picasso, 50 Years of his Work* (1946) Alfred H. Barr gives a bibliography of books and articles on Picasso. They number no less than 538, and many more have, of course, appeared since then. As a first introduction, the following books are the most important: the book by Barr, just quoted, a collection of reproductions with explanatory texts; and the book by Frank Elgar and Robert Maillard, published in 1956. A comprehensive iconography of paintings and drawings, but excluding graphic prints, will be found in Christian Zervos, *Pablo Picasso* (11 volumes have appeared up to now, 1932–60). Maurice Gieure's *Initiation à l'œuvre de Picasso*, 1951, is a very detailed aesthetic-scientific analysis. Jaime Sabartés, *Picasso, portraits et sou-* venirs, 1946 (English edition 1949) describes the artist's personality. Alexandre Cirici-Pellicer, *Picasso avant Picasso*, 1950, deals with his early period, before he settled in Paris, Bernhard Geiser's excellent catalogue, *Picasso peintre-graveur*, 1933, reproduces all early graphic works; it is to be hoped that a continuation dealing with the later prints will be published before long. Mourlot, *Picasso lithographe* (3 vols., 1949–56) reproduces the lithographs with all their states, which are particularly important in the case of Picasso. Geiser's later book, *L'Oeuvre gravée de Picasso*, 1955, contains a summary survey of Picasso's graphic work on 168 plates. Wilhelm Boeck's comprehensive work, *Picasso*, 1955, gives a detailed analysis of the oeuvre on 524 quarto pages of text (with more than 6 pages of bibliography) and 596 reproductions, but Picasso's work as illustrator is hardly mentioned. The problems of Picasso's early work have been discussed with a truly poetical insight by Theodor Däubler in a brief, but very penetrating analysis, reprinted in *Der neue Standpunkt*, 1957, pp. 125–39.

3. *Picasso et ses amis*, 1931, p. 180.

4. *Picasso, portraits et souvenirs*, p. 97.

5. *Arte Joven* means 'Young Art'. The aims of this periodical were similar to those of *Ver Sacrum*, published in Vienna.

6. Cf. Alexandre Cirici-Pellicer, *Picasso avant Picasso*, 1950, pp. 85 ff.

7. Reproduced by Cirici-Pellicer, p. 43, who identifies the persons portrayed as: Romeu (the owner of the restaurant), Picasso, Rocarol, Fontbona, A. Soto and Sabartés.

8. All original graphic prints used as illustrations before 1932 are reproduced in B. Geiser, *Picasso peintre-graveur*, 1933. This book will therefore not be quoted below unless for some special reason and we shall refer only to reproductions to be found elsewhere.

9. Reproduced in the catalogue of the Zürich Kunsthaus, *Pablo Picasso, Das graphische Werk*, 1954, plate 7.

10. Reproduced in the catalogue of the Zürich Kunsthaus, plate 8.

10a. Reproduced in the catalogue of the Museum of Fine Arts, Boston, 1961, *The Artist and the Book, 1860–1960 in Western Europe and the United States*, p. 153.

11. Reproduced in Pierre Mornand and J. R. Thomé, *Vingt artistes du livre*, 1950, p. 224.

12. U. E. Johnson, *Ambroise Vollard éditeur 1867–1939, an Appreciation and Catalogue*, New York, 1944.

13. A few examples: 'La mission de l'art n'est pas de copier la nature, mais de l'exprimer.' — 'La forme est . . . un truchement pour se communiquer des idées, des sensations, une vaste poésie.' (Picasso himself once said that a picture had to be understood in the same way as a poem.) — 'En partant du point extrême où vous arrivez, on fait peut-être d'excellente peinture,' Frenhofer says to Pourbus. — ' . . . nature artiste, cette nature folle à laquelle tant de pouvoirs sont confiés, et qui trop souvent en abuse, emmenant la froide raison, les bourgeois et même quelques amateurs à travers mille routes pierreuses, où, pour eux, il n'y a rien; tandis que, folâtre en ses fantaisies, cette fille aux ailes blanches y découvre des épopées, des châteaux, des œuvres d'art.' Such quotations could be multiplied.

14. Alfred H. Barr, *Picasso, 50 Years of his Work*, 1946, p. 145.

15. Maurice Gieure, *Initiation à l'œuvre de Picasso*, 1951.

16. Page 144, cf. also p. 121.

17. This hypothesis is seriously put forward by Thomé in Pierre Mornand and J. R. Thomé, *Vingt artistes du livre*, 1950, p. 230.

18. All thirteen etchings, as well as the title-page and the colophon, are reproduced in Bernhard Geiser, *Picasso peintre-graveur 1899–1931*, Berne, 1933 (Nos. 123–35). The etchings have also been published as a suite of loose prints with a special title-page, printed on large paper in an edition of ninety-nine copies signed by the artist. This title-page is decorated with a woodcut vignette after a drawing by Picasso (also reproduced by Geiser), which is not identical with the vignette on the title-page of the book.

Reproductions of one of the line drawings from the sixteen 'introductory' pages and of one etching in greatly reduced size in Elgar and Maillard, *Picasso*, pp. 151 and 159.

19. In addition to these 30 etchings (Nos. 143–72), Geiser reproduces another 19 etchings (Nos. 173–91), which were not used in the book. The opening of Book III is reproduced in the Catalogue Boston 1961, *The Artist and the Book 1860–1960 in Western Europe and the United States*, p. 155, the full page illustration from the same Book in the Catalogue of the Kunsthalle Bremen 1961, *Picasso: Druckgraphik, Gemälde, Handzeichnungen, Plastik*, p. 40.

20. *Cahiers d'Art*, 1930, pp. 511 ff.; cf. ib. 1931, p. 369 with reproductions.

21. Geiser describes a specimen copy which the publisher exhibited in New York in 1931. It was printed on Imperial Japanese paper and contained twenty-seven original designs by the artist, five different complete suites of proof etchings, four of them with remarques, a series of proofs of seventeen rejected plates and lastly three different proofs of an eighteenth etching, which was also rejected.

22. The six etchings are reproduced in the catalogue of the Musée Rath, Geneva, *L'œuvre gravée de Pablo Picasso*, 1954–5, plates 1–6. The full-page etchings have also been published in a portfolio with a special title-page: New York, The Print Club 1934, 150 numbered copies, size 38 × 28·5 cm., each print

signed. The title-page has as vignette a head after a drawing by Picasso.

23. Alfred H. Barr, *Picasso, 50 Years of his Work*, New York, 1946, p. 192.

24. *Picasso*, 1955, p. 188.

25. *Picasso, portraits et souvenirs*, pp. 130 f.

26. ib., pp. 169–73.

27. Year 10, 1935, pp. 185 ff. and 225 ff.; Year 13, 1938, pp. 3 ff. and 156 f. English translations of the poems have appeared in *Contemporary Poetry and Prose*, August 1936, and in *London Bulletin 1939*, Nos. 15–16. The original Spanish versions have been published in Mexico in 1944. (The last three references are taken from Barr, p. 287.) German translation by Paul Celan, with the French text opposite, in *Pablo Picasso, Wort und Bekenntnis*, Zürich, 1954.

28. All four etchings reproduced in the catalogue of the Musée Rath, plates 13–16.

29. *Picasso, portraits et souvenirs*, p. 138.

30. ib., p. 140.

31. Reproductions: monkey and bull in Mornand-Thomé, pp. 230–1; wasp and dragon-fly in the catalogue of the Zürich Kunsthaus, plates 77–8; ram and dragon-fly in the catalogue of the Musée Rath, plates 17–18; ostrich and hen in Geiser (1955), pls. 110–11; lobster in the Catalogue Boston 1961, *The Artist and the Book 1860–1960 in Western Europe and the United States*, p. 159.

Notes

32. In the years 1918–22, the German bibliophile publisher Hans von Weber published several books which, according to him, were illustrated with 'autograph zinc drawings' ('Urzinkzeichnungen'): 35th and 38th Hundertdruck; 5th, 8th, 11th, 13th, 16th to 19th Dreiangeldruck. This was probably the same or a similar technique.

33. Preface p. 15: 'Pour complaire à quelques amateurs de belle typographie, j'ai extrait des "Odes" de Sappho, aimablement mises à ma disposition par la Bibliothèque Nationale Suisse, quatorze poèmes qui n'ont aucun rapport avec l'art de Terpsychore. . . .'

34. Reproduced in Pierre Mornand and J. R. Thomé, *Vingt artistes du livre*, 1950, p. 228; in the catalogue of the Musée Rath, plate 21; by Geiser, 1955, plate 112; and in Elgar and Maillard, *Picasso*, p. 208.

35. English translation by Bernard Frechtman, 'Desire Caught by the Tail', London, Rider and Co., 1950.

36. Greatly reduced reproduction in Celan, p. 61.

37. *Messages Nr. 2.*

38. Three of these portraits reproduced in Mornand-Thomé, pp. 232 and 236.

39. Reproduced in the catalogue of the Musée Rath, plate 23.

40. Reproduced in the catalogue of the Musée Rath, plate 24.

41. The four etchings of the French edition reproduced ib. plates 25–8.

42. *Gedichte eines Gefühllosen*, by Carl Georg von Maassen under the pseudonym Tobias Schnellpfeffer, later with illustrations by Th. Th. Heine.

43. The portrait of Gongora and three other heads reproduced in the catalogue of the Musée Rath, plates 29–32; Sonnet III reproduced in the catalogue of the Kunsthalle Bremen, 1961, p. 41.

44. About the same time Picasso etched another, no less superb portrait of Gongora, quoted in the catalogue of the exhibition of his graphic work in the Zürich Kunsthaus, May-June 1954, No. 316.

45. Article on Picasso's *Gongora* in *Graphis* No. 24, 1948, pp. 310–19. See also the same author's *Etching and Engraving, Techniques and the Modern Trend*, London and New York, 1953, pp. 129–33, with reproductions of two *Gongora* heads.

46. Reproduced in the catalogue of the Musée Rath, plate 34.

47. J. R. Thomé in Mornand and Thomé, *Vingt artistes du livre*, pp. 234 f., with reproductions of three openings from this work. Two further pages are reproduced in the catalogue of the Musée Rath, plates 35 and 36.

48. Reproduced in Geiser, 1955, plate 135.

49. All reproduced in the catalogue of the Musée Rath, plates 41–3.

50. Reproduced in Mourlot, *Picasso lithographe* III (1956), p. 32.

51. This fly-title and another reproduced in the catalogue of the Musée Rath, plates 47 and 48.

52. Reproduced ib., plate 46.

53. All lithographs reproduced in the

catalogue of the Musée Rath, plates 49–57, and in Mourlot, *Picasso lithographe* III (1956), pp. 45–7.

54. In the catalogue of the Musée Rath (plate 55), the title lithograph is reproduced without the lettering and a comparison with the title-page in the book shows that the print has clearly been composed with a view to the words being inserted: without them it looks quite incomplete. The title-page with its lettering is reproduced in the Catalogue Boston 1961, *The Artist and the Book 1860–1960*, p. 161.

55. Reproduced in the catalogue of the Musée Rath, plate 58.

56. Reproduced in the catalogue of the Musée Rath, plate 61.

57. All fourteen prints are reproduced in Mourlot, *Picasso lithographe* III (1956), pp. 18–31. See also the reproduction in the Catalogue Boston 1961, p. 162.

58. The history of the poem is alluded to by Iliazd in a postscript entitled 'Adieu d'Iliazd à Grey': 'Jamais nous n'étions guidés par l'espoir que les soins apportés à la mise de votre œuvre puissent racheter l'hésitation passée. Délibérément nous avons tenté l'impossible. Et puis avec tout le mal que nous avons enduré contrariés et fatigués à l'infini dans la poursuite de l'achèvement de notre enterprise maintes fois défaite nous ne pûmes la continuer qu'en faisant calmer les blessures par cette illusion transparente que la patience est le souverain remède. Car nous n'avons pas désappris que vivre d'élans voués à l'echec est propre à la poésie et cherchâmes à persuader nous-mêmes mais en passant que nous étions encore à l'époque toute proche et déjà effroyablement lointaine où les poètes vivaient parmi nous.'

58a. See reproduction in the Catalogue Boston 1961, p. 164–5.

58b. One of the etchings is reproduced in the catalogue Kunsthalle Bremen 1961, p. 46.

59. ... Il poursuivait cet idéal de perfection dans le dessin qui a été le but de sa vie. 'Je ne sais pas si je suis un grand peintre, mais je suis un grand dessinateur. ...'

60. The poem reads:

Doucement pour dormir à l'ombre de
  l'oubli
ce soir
je tuerai les rôdeurs
silencieux danseurs
de la nuit
et dont les pieds de velours noir
sont un supplice à ma chair nue,
un supplice doux comme l'aile des
  chauves souris
et subtil à porter l'effroi
dans les coins où la peau se fait crain-
  tive émue
pour mieux aimer, pour avoir peur
d'un autre corps et du froid.

Mais quel fleuve pour fuir ce soir ô ma
  raison?
C'est l'heure des mauvais garçons
l'heure des mauvais voyous.
Deux grands yeux d'ombre dans la
  nuit
seraient pour moi si doux, si doux.

110

Prisonnier des tristes saisons
je suis seul, un beau crime à lui
là bas, là bas à l'horizon,
quelque serpent peut-être et glacé de
* n'aimer point.*

Mais où coule, où coule au loin
le fleuve dont a besoin
pour fuir ce soir ma raison?
Sur les berges vont les filles,
leurs yeux sont las, leurs cheveux
* brillent.*

Je ne sais rien dire à ces filles
dont ils sont
les mauvais garçons,
dont ils sont
les fiers maquignons.

Je suis seul, un beau crime à lui
Deux grand yeux d'ombre dans la nuit
seraient pour moi si doux, si doux.

C'est l'heure des mauvais voyoux. [*sic*]

60a. Reproduced in the catalogue Boston 1961, p. 166.

61. *Picasso, portraits et souvenirs*, p. 140.

62. In Robert Rey, *Estampes*, 1950: 'Picasso, lequel change sans cesse en restant lui-même et embrasse toutes les formes, et tous les mondes ... Il y a eu ... d'étranges géométries, et d'aventureuses déformations, et des métamorphoses, et des machines, et des illusions théâtrales, une prodigieuse extension du répertoire spirituel, toutes les explorations et tous les jeux d'une imagination démiurgique.'

63. One copy of this *de luxe* edition was offered by the Paris bookseller Blaizot in his catalogue 314 of March 1960 under No. 7261. It had belonged at one time to Lise Deharnie, a friend of Eluard's.

64. The Balzac portrait in this book was chosen from a series of nine lithographs which Picasso had made on November 25 and December 7, 1952. The remaining eight portraits were published in 1957 by the Galerie Louise Leiris, Paris, in a portfolio entitled *balzacs en bas de casse et picasso sans majuscule* ('balzacs in lower case and picasso without capitals') with a preface by Michel Leiris.

65. Information kindly communicated by M. Jean Hugues.

Bibliography

THERE are several lists of the books containing illustrations by Picasso.

In the first place we must mention a work already referred to several times, *Picasso peintre-graveur* by Bernhard Geiser, 1933. This work is arranged chronologically and lists the books containing one or more original prints, all of which are reproduced. As it concludes with the year 1931, only the early works are listed.

In *Picasso, 40 Years of his Art*, New York, 1936, Monroe Wheeler includes a list of 34 items.

The first systematic bibliography was published by A. Pouterman in *Signature*, No. 14, May 1940, pp. 10–21, under the title *Books illustrated by Pablo Picasso, together with a Hand-List*. The author tried to discriminate by listing only those books which contain real illustrations or a frontispiece portrait 'drawn expressly for the book'. We are not convinced that all the frontispieces listed by Pouterman were in fact drawn specially for the books he lists and are inclined to rely on the testimony of Sabartés, quoted above, that the artist often chose from his extensive oeuvre drawings of much earlier date and allowed them to be published for the first time.

Barr's *Picasso, 50 Years of his Work*, 1946, contains a list compiled by William S. Lieberman, who made use of Monroe Wheeler's list, but now reaches a total of 64 items. He states explicitly: 'Many of the books listed contain prints or reproductions of drawings which Picasso obligingly provided for the purpose', i.e. not made specially as illustrations for these books.

A list of 67 titles is given by Pierre Mornand and J. R. Thomé in their book *Vingt artistes du Livre*, 1950, pp. 305 ff.

The catalogue of an exhibition of Picasso's graphic work held in the Kunsthaus, Zürich, in May and June 1954 has an introduction by Bernhard Geiser, who also contributed a 'list of books illustrated with original graphic works', comprising 52 titles (Catalogue Nos. 434–85). Nine of the 110 reproductions show illustrations and frontispieces of various books (Nos. 7, 8, 16, 19, 21, 77, 78, 79, 83).

The same list, with 8 additional titles, appears also in Geiser's book *L'œuvre gravée de Picasso*, 1955. Of the 168 plates of this book, twenty reproduce book illustrations: plates 14, 15, 42–51, 57, 110–12, 114, 115, 135, 151.

Shortly after the Zürich exhibition, Picasso's graphic work was exhibited in the Musée Rath in Geneva (December 11, 1954 — January 31, 1955) and in the exhibition catalogue Maurice Bridel has compiled a list of the books illustrated by Picasso, likewise confined to books with original graphic prints. Bridel has divided the material into seven groups: illustrated books (Nos. i–xxiv); books of which the *éditions de luxe* contain several prints, the ordinary editions only one (No. xxv); books containing only one print (Nos. xxvi–xxxvii); books of which only the *édition de luxe* contains a print (Nos. xxxviii–lxi); one book illustrated by hand (No. lxii); one periodical with an original print (No. lxiii); one book in preparation (No. lxiv, Suarès, *Hélène chez Archimède*, which Vollard had planned as early as 1931). This catalogue contains 63 reproductions of book illustrations (plates 1–63).

Elgar and Maillard, *Picasso*, 1956, contains on pp. 307–8 a list of 58 'books illustrated with original contributions by Picasso', which contains nothing new. 'Original contributions' means, apparently original graphic prints.

At the end of 1956 an exhibition of books with illustrations by Picasso was held at the Galerie Matarasso in Nice. On this occasion H. Matarasso published a *Bibliographie des livres illustrés par Pablo Picasso. Œuvres graphiques 1905–1956*, Nice 1956, comprising 74 items on 18 pages. This bibliography, like that of Bridel, on which it is based, lists books containing one or more original prints.

Our own list, which follows below, was completed in January 1961 and is arranged as follows:

(A) Books containing illustrations which were either expressly made for the purpose or form such a close unity with the text that they are felt to be an integral part of the book.

(B) Books containing illustrations which were made independently of the text and were combined with it subsequently.

(C) Books containing a portrait of the author.

(D) Books containing a frontispiece which has no connection with the text.

(E) Books with a wrapper design.

(F) Miscellaneous.

A grouping of the books according to the technique employed for the illustrations seemed not appropriate in our context. We specify the technique in all cases in which it could be ascertained, but some of the books containing a single illustration were not available for inspection and had to be quoted at second hand from one of the lists mentioned above. For the sake of brevity we have used the term 'etching' to cover all types of copper engraving, whether dry-point, etching proper, aquatint, or a kindred method.

We have listed only those books in which the illustrations accompany a work of literature. In contrast to the exhibition catalogues mentioned, we have no reason here to make the inclusion of a work in our bibliography dependent upon the printing process employed. For this reason we have omitted such books as *Du cubisme* by Gleizes and Metzinger, 1947, in which an old etching by Picasso (Geiser No. 42) as well as prints by other artists are used to clarify the nature of cubism, nor do we list the Picasso monographs by Zervos (1926), George (1926), Level (1928), Ors (1930), Eluard (1944), Sabartés (1958), and Verdet's description of the sculpture 'La Chèvre' (1952), all of which have also been published in *éditions de luxe* with a Picasso print. (The etching to 'La Chèvre' is reproduced in the catalogue of the Musée Rath, plate 60.)

A. BOOKS CONTAINING ILLUSTRATIONS WHICH FORM
AN EVIDENT UNITY WITH THE TEXT

JACOB, Max. *Saint Matorel*. Illustré d'eaux-fortes par Pablo Picasso. [Publisher's mark.] Paris, Henry Kahnweiler, éditeur, 28, rue Vignon, 28.

Imprint: 11.2.1911. 100 numbered copies: 1–15 on Japanese Shidzucka, 16–100 on Van Gelder. In addition, i–iv as voucher copies, 0 and 00 as copyright copies for the Bibliothèque Nationale with prints of destroyed plates.

With 4 etchings. [A1

COCTEAU, Jean. *Le Coq et l'arlequin*. Notes autour de la musique. Avec un portrait de l'auteur et 2 monogrammes par P. Picasso. Paris, Éditions de la Sirène, 1918. (Coll. des Tracts. No. 1.)

Éditions de luxe: 1–5 on Chinese paper, 6–55 on Dutch deckle-edged paper.

With 2 drawings. [A2

OVIDIUS. Ovide. *Les Métamorphoses*. Eaux-fortes originales de Picasso. Lausanne, Albert Skira, éditeur, 1931.

Imprint: 25.10.1931. 145 numbered and signed copies: 1–5 on hand-made white Japanese paper with a suite of the etchings on Japanese paper with remarques in bistre and a second suite on Chinese paper with remarques in black, 6–30 on the same Japanese paper with a suite on Japanese paper with remarques in black, 31–125 on pure rag Arches paper, i–xx voucher copies.

With 30 etchings. [A3

ARISTOPHANES. *Lysistrata*. A new version by Gilbert Seldes with a special introduction by Mr Seldes and illustrations by Pablo Picasso, 1934. The Limited Editions Club, 1934.

Imprint: 1500 numbered and signed copies.

Contains 6 etchings and 34 reproductions of drawings from line blocks. [A4

ELUARD, Paul. *Divers poèmes du livre ouvert*. 18.4.1941. Fifteen copies written out by the poet, with illuminations from Picasso's hand. [A5

HUGNET, Georges. *Non vouloir*. Illustré de quatre gravures par Pablo Picasso. Éditions Jeanne Bucher, Paris 1942.

Imprint: 1.4.1942. 426 numbered copies: 1–20 on laid deckle-edged Arches, signed by the poet and by the illustrator, with a suite of the illustrations printed in colour and in colour and black, and with an original etching. 21–420 on featherweight paper, i–vi archive copies on laid deckle-edged Arches.

With 4 autograph zinc drawings. [A6

(PICASSO.) *Le Désir attrapé par la queue*. (Paris 1944. Edition of about 35 copies.) Photo-litho reproduction of Picasso's autograph, with frontispiece and 4 drawings. A trade edition in letterpress, in greatly reduced size, and one drawing omitted was published in 1945 by Gallimard, Paris.　　[A7

REVENTOS, Ramon. *Dos contes*. El centaure picador. El capvespre d'un faune, de Ramon Reventós (Moni). Gravats por Pablo Picasso. Editorial Albor. Paris-Barcelona 1947.

Imprint: Spring 1947. 250 numbered copies: 1–20 with, 21–250 without a suite of the etchings. Additional voucher copies.

With 4 etchings.　　[A8

REVENTOS, Ramon. *Deux contes*. Le centaure picador. Le crépuscule d'un faune. De Ramon Reventós (Moni). Gravures de Pablo Picasso. Éditions Albor. 1947.

Imprint: Summer 1947. 250 numbered copies: 1–20 with a suite of the etchings, 21–250 without the suite.

With 4 etchings.　　[A9

GONGORA

Imprint: 30.9.1948. 275 numbered copies: 1–5 on Imperial Japanese paper with a suite of 41 etchings on Chinese paper and of the etched text pages in the first state, 6–15 on specially made deckle-edged Marais with the same suite, 16–250 on the same paper without the suite, i–xxv for those who collaborated, of which five with the suite of the etched text pages in the first state.

First volume of the series 'Les grands peintres modernes et le livre'.

With etched title-page in calligraphy, 20 etched marginal drawings on the text pages, and 20 etchings.

　　[A10

REVERDY, Pierre. *Le Chant des morts*. *Poèmes*. Lithographies originales de Pablo Picasso. Tériade, Editeur.

Imprint: 30.9.1948. 270 numbered copies: 1–250 on wove deckle-edged Arches, i–xx not for the trade. All copies signed by the author.

With 126 illuminations in lithography.　　[A11

CÉSAIRE, Aimé. *Corps perdu*. Gravures de Pablo Picasso. Édition Fragrance, Paris.

Imprint: 3.6.1950. 219 numbered copies: 1–4 on Japanese deckle-edged paper with a suite of the 32 etchings on Chinese paper, 5–7 on Imperial Japanese paper with a suite on Chinese paper, 8–30 on specially made handmade Monval, with a suite of the prints on Japanese paper, 31–207 on the same paper without the suite, i–xii as voucher copies. All copies signed by the author and by the artist. With title in calligraphy, frontispiece, 10 fly-titles and 20 plates, all etched.

　　[A12

MONLUC, Adrien de, sous le nom de Guillaume de Vaux. *La Maigre*. Mise en lumière et en page par Iliazd. Illustré de pointes sèches par Pablo Picasso. Edité par le Degré quarante et un.

Imprint: 28.4.1952. Nos. i–xiv on

old deckle-edged Japanese paper, Nos. 1–52 on Chinese paper. 6 archive and 2 copyright copies.

With 8 etchings in the text and one etching on the cover.   [A13

GREY, Roch. *Chevaux de minuit*. Epopée. Aux bonnes soins du Degré quarante et un par Iliazd et Pablo Picasso. Cannes et Paris.

Imprint: 2. 3. 1956. 68 numbered copies, 1–52 on Japanese paper, i–xvi on Chinese paper.

With 12 etchings and one wrapper etching.   [A14

JACOB, Max. *Chronique des temps héroïques*, illustré par Pablo Picasso. Louis Broder.

'Ecrits et gravures', vol. 2. Imprint: Paris, October 1956. 170 copies on laid deckle-edged Monval. 1–150 and i–xx. Nos. 1–30 contain a suite on Japanese paper (title lithograph and the 3 etchings) in a lithographed cover.

With title lithograph, 3 etchings and 24 drawings engraved on wood by Aubert; title for the wrapper and decorated cover paper for the slip case in lithography.   [A15

(BENOIT, P. A.) *Picasso derrière le masque*. [Title on the wrapper.] *Poème*. Gravure de Picasso.

Imprint: Alès, January 1957. — 36 copies on handmade paper, signed by the author and by the artist.   [A16

TZARA, Tristan. *La rose et le chien, poème perpétuel*. Pablo Picasso. P. A. B[enoit].

Imprint: 22 copies, Alès, March 1958, the plates have been destroyed.

Contains three etchings. Signed by the author and by the artist.   [A17

BENOIT, P. A. *Pierres*. Picasso.

Imprint: Alès, May 1958. 3, 6 and 36 copies. With a Picasso etching as frontispiece. The first 3 copies contain two additional signed prints of the etching in red and blue, the next 6 copies one additional signed print of the etching in red. All copies signed by the author and by the artist.   [A18

CHAR, René. *L'escalier de Flore*. Picasso. PAB[enoit].

Imprint: Alès, May 1958. 36 and 4 copies. One etching; wrapper design by Picasso.   [A19

BENOIT, P. A. *Si large mon image*

Imprint: Alès, Dec. 31, 1958. 2 copies only, numbered I and II. Published by P. A. Benoit.   [A20

LE FRÈRE MENDIANT o Libro del Conocimiento. Los viajes en Africa publicados antiquamente por Bergeron Margry y Jimenez de la Espada e illustrados ahora y comaginados por Pablo Picasso e Iliazd. Latitud Cuarenta y uno. Se tiraron 54 ejemplares en japon antiguo numerados de 1 a 54.

Imprint: The 22 dry-point etchings were completed on April 23, 1958, the two etchings for the wrapper on May 8, 1959. The type set by Iliazd. The etchings printed by Roger Lacourière and Jacques Frélaut, the text printed by Imprimerie Union. The printing was finished on May 19, 1959.   [A21

BENOIT, P. A. *Meurs*. Picasso. [Lettering on wrapper.]

Alès [1960]. Imprint: 40 and 10

copies. With a frontispiece etched by Picasso. Miniature size. 32 mm. deep and 46 mm. wide. The imprint has the author's initials and the artist's signature. The 10 copies of the *de luxe* edition contain two prints each of the etching in black and red. [A22

BENOIT, P. A. *Vers où l'on voit.* Picasso. [Lettering on wrapper.]

Imprint: Alès, April 1960. 33 and 6 copies. All copies are numbered and signed by the author's hand. Each of the 6 copies of the *de luxe* edition contains two prints of the etching in different colours. [A23

ROQUE, Jacqueline. *Température.*

Imprint: Alès, P. A. B[enoit], 28 and 8 copies. Published June 1960. [A24

B. BOOKS CONTAINING ILLUSTRATIONS WHICH HAVE NO EVIDENT CONNECTION
WITH THE TEXT, AND SUITES TO WHICH TEXTS
HAVE BEEN ADDED SUBSEQUENTLY

JACOB, Max. *Le Siège de Jérusalem. Grande tentation céleste de Saint Matorel.* Illustré d'eaux-fortes par Pablo Picasso. [Publisher's mark.] Paris, Henry Kahnweiler, éditeur, 28, rue Vignon, 28.

Imprint: 21.1.1914. 100 numbered copies: 1–15 on Japanese Inteotukeo-ku, 16–100 on Van Gelder. In addition i–iv as voucher copies and 0 and 00 as copyright copies for the Bibliothèque Nationale with prints from the destroyed plates.

With 3 etchings. [B1

SALMON, André. *Le Manuscrit trouvé dans un chapeau.* Orné de dessins à la plume par Pablo Picasso. [Vignette.] Paris, Société Littéraire de France, 10, rue de l'Odéon, 10, 1919.

Imprint: 25.8.1919. 750 numbered copies on wove Lafuma paper.

With 38 drawings reproduced from line blocks. [B2

REVERDY, Pierre. *Cravates de chanvre.* Illustré d'eaux-fortes par Pablo Picasso. Éditions Nord-Sud, 12, rue Cortet, Paris.

Imprint: 22.3.1922. 125 numbered copies: 1–15 on Japanese paper, 16–30 on Van Gelder, 31–120 on ordinary paper. Also i–x as voucher copies, and 2 copyright copies for the Bibliothèque Nationale, marked 0 and 00.

The copies on Japanese and on Van Gelder paper contain 3 etchings, the others only one. [B3

BALZAC, Honoré de. *Le Chef-d'œuvre inconnu.* Eaux-fortes originales et dessins gravés sur bois de Pablo Picasso. Paris, Ambroise Vollard, éditeur, 1931.

Imprint: 12.11.1931. 305 copies: 1–65 on Imperial Japanese paper with a suite of the etchings on deckle-edged Rives; 66–305 on deckle-edged Rives, i–xxxv not for the trade.

With 16 pages of linear drawings, 67 drawings engraved on wood in the text and on the covers, 12 full-page etchings and a thirteenth etching as register. [B4

ELUARD, Paul. *La Barre d'appui.* Poèmes illustrés de trois eaux-fortes par Pablo Picasso. Éditions 'Cahiers d'Art'.

Imprint: 5.6.1936. 40 numbered copies on Imperial Japanese paper.

With 3 etchings. Nos. I–VI with three suites, in blue, green and red ink[63] (not mentioned in the colophon). [B5

ELUARD, Paul. *Les Yeux fertiles.* Avec un portrait et quatre illustrations par Pablo Picasso. G.L.M., 1936.

Imprint: 15.10.1936. 1500 copies: 1–10 on Imperial Japanese paper, with one etching, 11–60 on deckle-edged Pannekoek, 61–1300 on esparto paper, SP 1301–SP 1500 [Service de Presse] not for the trade.

Contains one portrait (pencil drawing reproduced in collotype) and 4 line illustrations (3 after etchings, one after a pen drawing). [B6

ILIAZD. *Afat.* Soixante-seize sonnets. Pablo Picasso. Six gravures originales sur cuivre. Le Degré quarante et un.

Imprint: letterpress printed from 2 to 30.3.1940; gravure (from the plates before steel-facing) from 4 to 8.12.1939. 50 numbered copies, and another 14 not for the trade: i–vi, 01–06, 0 and 00, all on deckle-edged Monval and all signed by the author and by the artist.

With 2 fly-titles in calligraphy and 4 plates of illustrations, all etched. [B7

BUFFON. *Eaux-fortes originales pour des textes de Buffon.* Martin Fabiani, éditeur à Paris, 1942.

Imprint: 26.5.1942. 226 numbered copies: one on old laid paper with a suite on old bluish deckle-edged paper, 2–6 on Japanese deckle-edged paper with a suite of the etchings on Chinese paper, 7–36 on Imperial Japanese paper with a suite on Chinese paper, 37–91 on wove deckle-edged Montval, 92–226 on wove Vidalon.

With 31 etchings. [B8

HUGNET, Georges. *La Chèvre-feuille* avec six gravures de Pablo Picasso. Robert J. Godet, éditeur, 1943.

Imprint: 4.12.1943. 534 copies: 1–25 on wove deckle-edged Arches with a suite of the illustrations in colour and one original etching (earlier state), 26–525 without the suite. Further i–vi on deckle-edged Arches and three private copies on deckle-edged Arches-Bristol for the author, the illustrator and the publisher.

With 6 etchings. [B9

PICASSO, Pablo. *Grâce et mouvement.* 14 compositions originales gravées sur cuivre. Zürich, Grosclaude.

Imprint: 30.11.1943. 350 copies: 1–100 on Imperial Japanese paper, with a suite of the illustrations on Chinese paper, 101–350 on handmade paper. Also 300 numbered suites on deckle-edged paper in larger size. All copies signed by the publisher.

Contains 14 poems of Sappho and 14 plates etched by the firm of Haefeli & Cie, La Chaux-de-Fonds, after drawings by Picasso. [B10

JOURS DE GLOIRE. *Histoire de la libéra-tion de Paris*. (Paris, S.J.P.F., 1946.)

1000 numbered copies, and 50 on Lana paper not for the trade, of which 25 with the etching in an earlier state.

Contains on pp. 23–5 Paul Eluard's poem *Dans un miroir noir* with one etching and 2 drawings by Picasso.

[B11

[Russian:] IL'JAZD. [i.e. Il'ja Zdanevič.] *Pis'mo*. Pikasso, Gravjury. Sorok pervyj gradus.

Copyright: 1948. 66 copies: 1–50 on old Japanese paper. Not for the trade: HC 1–8 on eighteenth-century Dutch deckle-edged paper, HC 9–13 on Marais paper, 3 copies on parchment: for the author, the artist and the muse. Signed by the author and by the illustrator.

With 6 etchings, the title etching repeated on the parchment wrapper.

[B12

MERIMÉE, Prosper. Picasso. *Carmen*. Sur le texte de Prosper Mérimée. La Bibliothèque Française.

Imprint: 14.5.1949. 320 numbered copies: I–XI on Imperial Japanese paper, containing, in addition to the 38 etchings, another 4 aquatint prints and a suite of the etchings on Chinese paper, 1–289 on wove deckle-edged Monval, A–T on the same paper as voucher copies. All copies signed by Picasso. The copper plates have been destroyed.

With 30 full-page etchings, 4 etched initials and 4 etched vignettes.

[B13

GOLL, Yvan. *Elégie d'Iphétonga. Suivie de Masques de cendre*. Illustrés de quatre lithographies originales de Pablo Picasso. Éditions Hémisphères, Paris.

Imprint: 30.6.1949. 220 numbered copies: 1–20 on hand-made Arches with a suite of the lithographs on Japanese paper, 21–200 on hand-made Rives, i–xx as voucher copies.

With 4 lithographs. [B14

TZARA, Tristan. *De Mémoire d'homme*. Poème. Lithographies de Pablo Picasso. Bordes, éditeur.

Imprint: 25.10.1950. 350 numbered copies: 1–30 on Van Gelder with a suite of the lithographs on Japanese paper, signed by the author and by the artist, 31–330 on deckle-edged Arches, initialled by the author, HC i to HC xx voucher copies on esparto paper.

With 9 lithographs. [B15

PICASSO ET ELUARD. *Le Visage de la paix*. Paris, Éditions Cercle d'Art.

Imprint: October 1951. 2250 copies: I–CL on Johannot pure rag paper with an additional lithograph. 1–2100 on offset paper, of which the last 100 copies as voucher copies.

With 29 drawings; in the *édition de luxe* an additional lithograph. [B16

SATIE, Erik. *Cahiers d'un mammifère*. (*Extraits*.) Liège, aux éditions dynamo. P. Aelberts, éditeur. (Brimborions, 22.)

Imprint: August 1951. *Édition de luxe*: 40 copies on vellum paper, 10 on Dutch deckle-edged paper, one on Japanese paper, numbered 1–51.

Contains 3 pen drawings reproduced from line blocks. The author's portrait opposite the title-page is by A. Frueh.

[B17

TOESCA, Maurice. *Six contes fantasques* illustrés de six burins par Picasso. (Paris) Flammarion.

Imprint: 28.10.1953. 225 numbered copies: 1–25 on Imperial Japanese paper with a suite of the dry-point etchings on deckle-edged Auvergne, 26–100 on wove deckle-edged Montval, 101–200 on laid deckle-edged Arches, i–xxv (not for the trade). In addition, 30 suites of the etchings for the publisher's friends.

With 6 etchings. [B18

DIDEROT, Denis. *Mystification ou Histoire des portraits.* Préface de Pierre Daix. Texte et notes établis par Yves Benot. Illustration de Pablo Picasso. Les éditeurs français réunis, 33, rue Saint-André-des-Arts, Paris VI.

Copyright: 1954. 530 numbered copies: A–E on Japanese deckle-edged paper, I–XCV on wove deckle-edged Arches, 1–430 on wove pure rag Lafuma paper; (401–30 not for the trade).

With 4 drawings. [B19

LAPORTE, Geneviève. *Les Cavaliers d'ombre.* 7 illustrations de Pablo Picasso. Gravures sur cuivre de Georges Bétemps. Préface de Jacques Audiberti. Paris, J. Foret.

Imprint: 25.6.1954. 217 numbered copies: A–Q on deckle-edged Montval-Auvergne with 2 suites, one in black on Japanese paper, the other in sepia on Arches paper, I–L on pure rag Arches with a suite on Japanese paper in black, 1–50 on Marais with a suite in sepia, 51–150 on Johannot. All copies signed by the publisher.

With 7 drawings reproduced as etchings. [B20

TZARA, Tristan. *A haute flamme.* Pablo Picasso.

Imprint: 20.4.1955. 70 numbered copies on deckle-edged Japanese paper, signed by the author and by the artist.

With 5 etchings and an etched title on the wrapper. [B21

SUARÈS, André. *Hélène chez Archimède.* Illustrations de Pablo Picasso. Nouveau Cercle Parisien du Livre, 1955.

Imprint: 6.10.1955. 240 numbered copies: 1–140 for members of the society, I–C for the trade.

With 22 drawings (engraved on wood by Aubert). [B22

BENOIT, P.A. *Autre chose.* PAB.

Imprint: 1956. 35 copies, Nos. 1–30 and 5 not for the trade, all on deckle-edged Arches signed by the author. Published by P. A. Benoit, Alès. The etched frontispiece signed by Picasso.

With one etching by Picasso. [B23

CREVEL, René. *Nuit.* Picasso. PAB (title on wrapper).

Imprint: May 1956. 30 copies.

Published by P. A. Benoit, Alès (Gard), in miniature size (65 mm. high, 90 mm. wide).

Etched frontispiece (29 mm. high, 49 mm. wide). [B24

DAUVEN, Jean. *Jean Cocteau chez les sirènes*. Une expérience de linguistique sur le discours de réception à l'Académie française de M. Jean Cocteau. Illustrations de Picasso. Monaco, Éditions du Rocher, 1956.

On pp. 90–2 reproductions of a series of three pen drawings, which have nothing in common with the text except a satirical tendency.   [B25

CHAR, René. *Pourquoi la journée vole*.
Imprint: Alès, July 1960. 25 copies. Published by P. A. Benoit.   [B26

BENOIT, P. A. *Toute la vie*. Picasso.
Imprint: Alès, August 1960. 50 copies on deckle-edged Arches paper numbered by hand 1 to 44 and I to VI and signed by the author. Published by P. A. Benoit. The etched frontispiece signed by Picasso.   [B27

C. BOOKS WITH ONE OR MORE PORTRAITS OF THE AUTHOR

APOLLINAIRE, Guillaume. *Alcools*. Paris, Mercure de France, 1908.

Only a part of the edition contains a portrait of the author in half-tone. Second edition 1913.   [C1

APOLLINAIRE, Guillaume. *Calligrammes*. Poèmes de la paix et de la guerre. (1913–16). Ondes — Etendards — Case d'armons — Lueurs de tirs — Obus couleur de lune — La tête étoilée. Avec un portrait de l'auteur par Pablo Picasso gravé sur bois par R. Jandon. Paris, Mercure de France, 1918.

Éditions de luxe: 1–4 on Imperial Japanese paper with a second portrait of the author etched by Jandon after a drawing by Picasso, 5–37 on deckle-edged Arches. A–C on Chinese paper, not for the trade. Reprinted several times, most recently in 1955 by the Club du meilleur livre.   [C2

VALÉRY, Paul. *La jeune parque*. Avec un portrait de l'auteur en lithographie par Pablo Picasso. Éditions de la Nouvelle Revue française. Paris, 35, 37, rue Madame, 1920.

Nos. I–XXV not for the trade. Nos. 1–500 on deckle-edged Arches.

With a portrait of the author in photo-litho.   [C3

SALMON, André. *Peindre*. Avec un portrait inédit de l'auteur par Pablo Picasso. Paris, Aux Éditions de la Sirène.

Imprint: 20.9.1921. 900 numbered copies. 1–40 on Korean felt paper, 41–900 on pure rag Lafuma paper.

The portrait is a pencil drawing reproduced in collotype.   [C4

HUIDOBRO, Vincent. *Saisons choisies*. Poèmes, La Cible, 1921.

Portrait of the author in heliogravure.   [C5

PARNAK, Valentin. *Karabkaetsya akrobat*. [Poems in Russian.] Paris, Franko-russkaya pečat', 1922.

Portrait of the author in heliogravure.   [C6

BILLY, André. *Apollinaire vivant*. Avec une photographie inédite et des portraits-charges de Pablo Picasso. Éditions de la Sirène, 28, Boulevard Malesherbes, à Paris, 1923.

With 2 portrait caricatures of Apollinaire. [C7

BRETON, André. *Clair de terre*. Avec un portrait par Picasso, 1923. (Collection Littérature.)

Imprint: 15.11.1923. 240 copies: I–III on Chinese paper, IV–XIII on Japanese paper, XIV–XXXVIII on Dutch paper, 2 copies, marked G, on 'Geranium' paper, 200 copies on offset paper.

In the 40 *de luxe* copies, the portrait of the author is an original etching, in the others a reproduction. [C8

COCTEAU, Jean. *Le Secret professionnel*. Paris, Delamain . . . Stock 1924. On the reverse of the title-page a portrait of the author, from a line-block after a pen drawing. [C9

CANUDO. *S.P. 503. Le Poème du Vardar suivi de la Sonate à Saloniques* avec un image de l'auteur par Picasso et un frontispice musical de Maurice Ravel. Ex-libris de Lambert. Paris, 78, Boulevard Saint-Michel, 1928.

Nos. 1–250 on ordinary paper, Nos. A–E on 'papier de grand luxe'. [C10

JACOB, Max. *Le Cornet à dés*. Paris, Librairie Stock, 1923. (Les Contemporains.)

On the wrapper: Édition complète revue et corrigée par l'auteur.

Édition de luxe: 50 numbered copies on deckle-edged Van Gelder. [C11

FAURE, Elie. *Napoléon*. Portrait dessiné par Pablo Picasso. Paris, Les Éditions G. Crès & Cie, 1924. (Maîtres et jeunes d'aujourd'hui.) [C12

RADIGUET, Raymond. *Les Joues en feu*, Poèmes anciens et modernes inédits 1917–21 précédés d'un portrait de Pablo Picasso et d'un poème de Max Jacob . . . F. Paillart. Paris, Bernard Grasset, 1925.

Imprint: 8.7.1925. 1370 numbered copies as 'édition originale'. Nos. I–XX on Chinese paper, XXI–LXX on Japanese paper, LXXI–CCXLV on Dutch deckle-edged paper, CCXLVI–CCLXX on Madagascar **paper** — all these with a suite on Chinese paper. Nos. 1–1100 on Lafuma paper.

The portrait is a drawing reproduced in collotype. [C13

REVERDY, Pierre. *Ecumes de la mer* avec un portrait de Picasso gravé sur bois par G. Aubert. Paris, Éditions de la Nouvelle Revue Française, 1925.

Imprint: 9.6.1925. 831 copies: A–O on old Japanese paper, I–LXVI (not for the trade) and 1–750 on Navarre paper. [C14

APOLLINAIRE, Guillaume. *Contemporains pittoresques*. En frontispice, un portrait de l'auteur par Picasso. Paris, Les Éditions de la Belle Page. (Le Livre Neuf, 3.)

Imprint: 18.1.1929. Nos. 1–15 on Imperial Japanese paper, 1635 on Van Gelder, 36–340 on Arches. Nos. i–xx on various papers. [C15

REVERDY, Pierre. *Sources du vent 1915–1929*. Avec un portrait par Picasso reproduit en fac-similé. Paris, Maurice Sachs, 1929.

116 numbered copies: one on white

Japanese paper, 2–6 on old deckle-edged Japanese paper, 7–16 on Imperial Japanese paper, 17–96 on Van Gelder, i–xx not for the trade.　　[C16

AIMOT, J. M. *Mané-Katz*. Préface de Paul Fierens. Paris, Marcel Seheur, 1933.

'L'Art et la vie'. With a portrait of Mané-Katz.　　　　　　　[C17

WEILL, Berthe. *Pan! dans l'œil!* . . . Avec une préface de Paul Reboux. Orné des aquarelles et dessins de Raoul Dufy, Pascin et Picasso. Paris, Librairie Lipschutz, 1933.

530 numbered copies. I–V on Japanese paper, not for the trade, VI–XXX on Van Gelder, 1–500 on deckle-edged Marais.

In addition to the frontispiece portrait, the book contains a second drawing by Picasso, entitled 'Composition', not connected with the text.　　　　　　　　　　　[C18

ELUARD, Paul. *Sur les pentes inférieures*. (Paris, La Peau de Chagrin [1941].) (Collection 'Poètes'.)

Brochure of 8 pages, without title-page. At the head of the first page a portrait of the author, a pen drawing reproduced from a line block.　　[C19

ELUARD, Paul. *Au rendez-vous allemand*. Paris, Éditions de Minuit, 1944.

Imprint: 15.12.1944. 120 numbered copies on rag paper. 1–20 (imprint signed by Picasso) contain the portrait as etching, 21–120 as half-tone after the etching.

The copy we inspected was that of the well-known Paris master-binder Paul Bonet and contained also an autograph letter from Eluard, two poems from the book in holograph and other items relating to the book.　[C20

APOLLINAIRE, Guillaume. *Les Mamelles de Tirésias* avec six portraits inédits par Picasso. Paris, Éditions du Bélier, 1946.

Imprint: 30.4.1946. 456 copies: 1–400 and I–XXX on Malacca paper, A–Z on deckle-edged Arches. In addition a few voucher copies.

The 6 portraits are caricature pen drawings reproduced in collotype.　　　　　　　　　　　[C21

APOLLINAIRE, Guillaume. *Ombre de mon amour*. Avec de nombreux documents et dessins inédits et un portrait d'Apollinaire par Picasso. Vésenaz-Genève, Pierre Cailler, 1948.

The frontispiece is a drawing reproduced in half-tone. The third edition of the book was the first to contain the portrait by Picasso.　　　[C22

MALLARME, Stéphane. *Lettres et poèmes inédits*. Précédés d'une lettre inédite de Paul Valéry. Hors-texte Stéphane Mallarmé par Pablo Picasso. Quatrain à Méry Laurent. Paris, Librairie Les Lettres, 1948.

Offprint of the special number of the periodical 'Les Lettres' in 150 numbered copies. I–XV on deckle-edged Van Gelder, 1–135 on Marais paper.

The portrait is a drawing reproduced in half-tone.　　　　　[C23

THOREZ, Maurice. *Fils du peuple*. Portrait de l'auteur par Picasso, illustrations du texte par Amblard, Auricoste,

Fongeron, Milhau, Pignon, et Tas-
litzky. Paris, Éditions sociales.

Imprint: 15.2.1950. *Édition de
luxe*: 50 numbered copies on Lafuma
paper. [C24

SATIE, Erik. *L'Eloge des critiques*. Liège,
Aux Éditions Dynamo, P. Aelberts,
éditeur. (Brimborions, 13.)

Imprint: October 1950. *Édition de
luxe*: 40 copies on vellum paper, and
11 on Madagascar paper, numbered
1–51. [C25

APOLLINAIRE, Guillaume. *Lettres à
Jane Mortier*. Liège, Aux Éditions
Dynamo, P. Aelberts, éditeur. (Brim-
borions, 14.)

Imprint: 9.11.1950. *Édition de luxe*:
40 copies on vellum paper and 11 on
Madagascar paper, numbered 1–51.
[C26

APOLLINAIRE, Guillaume. *Le Guetteur
mélancolique*. Préface d'André Salmon.
Frontispice de Picasso. (Paris,) NRF,
Gallimard.

Imprint: 3.6.1952. 1545 numbered
copies: Nos. 1–20 and A–F on Madagascar, Nos. 21–70 and G–M on Dutch
deckle-edged paper, Nos. 71–470 and
N–Z on pure rag Lafuma-Navarre
paper, Nos. 471–1520 on Navarre-
Voiron paper. (Copies A–Z and 1471–
1520 not for the trade.)

The portrait of Apollinaire is a
caricature. [C27

ROY, Claude. *Elégie des lieux communs*.
Récit-poème avec un portrait de
l'auteur et de Claire par Picasso.
(Limoges,) Rougerie (1952). (Poésie
et critique, 9.)

850 numbered copies: Nos. 1–250
on heavy, Nos. 251–850 on light Afnor
paper. Further copies A–J on deckle-
edged Lacombe paper, 5 copies on BFK
paper, not for the trade, marked HC.

With a double portrait of the author
and his wife. [C28

STRAWINSKY, Igor. *Poétique musicale*.
Avec un portrait de Picasso. Nouvelle
édition revue et complétée. Paris,
Éditions Le Bon Plaisir; Plon. (Amour
de la musique.)

Imprint: 15.4.1952.

The portrait is a drawing reproduced from a half-tone block. [C29

BALZAC, Honoré de. *Le Père Goriot*.
Préface de André Maurois de
l'Académie Française. Lithographie
originale de Picasso. Paris, Imprimerie
Nationale, André Sauret, éditeur.

(Collection du grand prix des meilleurs romans du 19e siècle, vol. 5.)

Imprint: 30.12.1952. Nos. I–CCC
on laid deckle-edged Arches with a
second impression of the lithograph on
Chinese paper, Nos. 1–3000 on wove
Arches paper, 100 copies, marked H.C.,
not for the trade. The Balzac portrait
opposite the title page is an offset
lithograph.[64] [C30

ELUARD, Paul. *Poésie ininterrompue II*.
(Paris,) NRF, Gallimard.

Imprint: 1953. *Édition de luxe*: 1–
15 and A–E on laid Dutch deckle-
edged paper, 16–140 and F–O on
Lafuma-Navarre rag paper.

The portrait is a pen drawing reproduced from a line block. [C31

(RADIGUET, Raymond.) *Le Diable au*

corps. (Paris, Le Club du meilleur livre.)

Imprint: 15.8.1953. 150 copies numbered I–CL and 5000 numbered 1–5000. The red chalk drawing is dated 17.12.20. [C32

SATIE, Erik. *Propos à propos.* Liège, Éditions Dynamo, P. Aelberts, éditeur. (Brimborions, 31.)

Imprint: December 1954. *Édition de luxe*: 40 copies on vellum paper, 10 copies on Dutch deckle-edged paper, and one copy on Japanese paper, numbered 1–51. [C33

SABATHIER LEVEQUE, Marc. *Oratorio pour la nuit de noel.* Illustré de seize portraits de l'auteur par Pablo Picasso. (Paris,) Les Éditions de Minuit.

Copyright: 1955. *Édition de luxe*: 1–11 and A–E on pure rag paper, 12–44 and F–I on esparto paper, 45–382 on vellum paper.

All the portraits, pen drawings reproduced from line blocks, are dated Perpignan, 26.8.54. [C34

PRÉVERT, Jacques. *Paroles.* Édition revue . . . Paris, NRF, 1956. The frontispiece, a portrait of Prévert, is a reproduction of a charcoal drawing by Picasso dated 25.9.56. The book was first published in 1949 without the portrait. This second edition is numbered 5101–7100 and h.c. (hors commerce) 7101–7150. [C35

ELUARD, Paul. *Poésies* choisies et présentées selon l'ordre chronologique par Claude Roy. Iconographie de Jean Hugues. (Paris, Club des meilleurs livres, 1959.)

Édition de luxe I–CL, ordinary edition 1–4700 with a portrait of the author by Picasso in 18 variations, all of 1952. [C36

D. BOOKS WITH A FRONTISPIECE (except Benoit editions)

SALMON, André. *Poèmes.* Paris, Edités par les soins de 'Vers et Proses', 1905.

Édition de luxe: about 10 copies (the exact number can no longer be ascertained) with a frontispiece etching by Picasso. [D1

JACOB, Max. *Le Cornet à dés.* Paris, l'auteur 1917.

Édition de luxe: 14 numbered copies containing an etching by Picasso. [D2

JACOB, Max. *Le Phanérogame.* Paris, l'auteur 1917.

Édition de luxe: 20 numbered copies on Japanese paper containing an etching on zinc. [D3

JACOB, Max. *La Défense de Tartufe.* Paris, Société Littéraire de France, 1919.

Édition de luxe: 25 numbered copies on Rives paper with an etching by Picasso. [D4

ARAGON, Louis. *Feu de joie.* Paris, Au Sans Pareil 1920. (Collection de Littérature.)

1070 copies: I–V on Japanese paper, VI–XV and A–E on deckle-edged Arches (these are on large paper); 1–1000 and 50 copies for the press (marked 000) on thick paper. [D5

GEORGE, Waldemar. *Picasso dessins.* Paris, Éditions de Quatre chemins, 1926.

Édition de luxe: 100 numbered copies with a lithograph. [D6

LEVEL, André. *Picasso.* Paris, G. Crès. (Les Cahiers d'aujourd'hui.)

Imprint: 1928. *Édition de luxe:* 120 numbered copies with a lithograph.

[D7

TZARA, Tristan. *L'Antitête.* Paris, Éditions des Cahiers Libres, 1933.

Edition of 1218 numbered copies. Only Nos. 1–15 and three private copies (for the author, the illustrator and the publisher) contain an etching by Picasso, printed by the artist himself on a handpress.[65] [D8

HUGNET, Georges. *Petite anthologie poétique du surréalisme.* Paris, Jeanne Bucher, 1934.

Édition de luxe: 28 numbered copies on Montval paper with one etching. For each copy of the book the plate was printed on a different paper, which is pasted on the text paper. Consequently all impressions vary in appearance. [D9

LEVINSON, André. *Serge Lifar. Destin d'un danseur.* Frontispice de P. Picasso. (Paris,) Éditions Bernard Grasset.

Imprint: 6.8.1934. 1930 copies: Nos. 1–70 and HC I–HC X on deckle-edged Arches, 1–1650 and 1–200 for the press on Navarre paper. The frontispiece is a reproduction of a drawing in Indian ink and wash, representing Lifar and Tatarin, dated Monte Carlo, April 1925. [D10

COCTEAU, Jean. *Orphée.* A Tragedy in One Act and an Interval. Translated by Carl Widman. London, Oxford University Press, 1933.

Édition de luxe: 100 numbered copies on Basingwork paper, signed by the author and by Picasso. The frontispiece is a half-tone reproduction of a drawing, which is stated on the reverse of the title-page to have been 'specially drawn by Pablo Picasso'. [D11

PERET, Benjamin. *De Derrière des fagots.* Paris, Éditions Surréalistes, José Corti, 1934.

Imprint: 16.8.1934. 599 numbered copies. Only Nos. 1–24 (on Japanese paper) contain an etching by Picasso. In some copies the artist coloured the prints by hand. [D12

CHAR, René. *Dépendance de l'adieu.* Avec un dessin de Picasso. Paris, Éditions G.L.M., 1936. (Repères. 14.)

Imprint: May 1936. 70 numbered copies on Normandy paper. The frontispiece is dated 13 janvier xxxvi (pen drawing reproduced by line block).

[D13

DECAUNES, Luc. *L'Indicatif présent ou l'infirme tel qu'il est.* Poèmes. Avec un frontispice de Pablo Picasso. Paris, Soutes, 1938.

Édition de luxe: 25 numbered copies and 5 voucher copies marked HC on Montval paper with a signed etching. [D14

ELUARD, Paul. *Solidarité.* Poème. Paris, G.L.M., 1938.

150 numbered copies. Contains one etching each by Picasso, Buckland-

Wright, Hayter, Husband, Masson, Miro and Tanguy. All prints signed. [D15

BRETON, André. *Anthologie de l'humour noir*. Paris, Éditions du Sagittaire, 1940.

The *édition de luxe* contains an etching signed by Picasso: 3 copies on Imperial Japanese paper, 10 on deckle-edged Van Gelder, 35 on pure rag paper. Not for the trade: 2 on Japanese paper, 2 on deckle-edged paper, 5 on pure rag paper. According to Matarasso, the etching is not signed in the copies on Japanese paper (probably owing to war conditions). [D16

MABILLE, Pierre. *Le Miroir du merveilleux*. Paris, Éditions du Sagittaire, 1940.

Édition de luxe: 12 copies on Lafuma paper and 7 on esparto paper (not for the trade) with an etching by Picasso. [D17

DESNOS, Robert. *Contrée*. Eau-forte de Picasso. Robert J. Godet. Paris 1944.

Imprint: 31.5.1944. 213 copies: 3 private copies on hand-made Arches paper for the author, the illustrator and the publisher, I–X on the same paper with a set of proofs of the etching in black, of the states in colour, and of the destroyed plate. 1–200 on wove pure rag Lafuma paper. With one etching, dated 23 D(écembre) 43, and 23 vignettes from line blocks (some repeated) after sections of the etching. [D18

CHAR, René. *Le Marteau sans maître*, 1927–35. Version définitive. Paris, Libraire José Corti, 1945.

Édition de luxe: Nos. 1–25 on deckle-edged Arches with an etching by Picasso. [D19

ELUARD, Paul. *Une longue réflexion amoureuse*. Frontispice de Picasso. Neuchâtel et Paris. Ides et Calendes.

Imprint: 17.11.1945. 1550 copies for the trade: Nos. 1–50 on hand-made paper, Nos. 51–1550 on white esparto paper. In addition, not for the trade: 10 private copies on deckle-edged paper, 50 on white esparto paper, 50 review copies for the press. The frontispiece is a pencil drawing of a girl's portrait, dated 28 Août xxxvi, reproduced in collotype on calendered Chinese paper. [D20

RIFFAUD, Madeleine. *Le Poing fermé*. Avec un frontispice de Pablo Picasso et une préface de Paul Eluard. Paris, L'ancolie. (Tel est mon plaisir, 4.)

Imprint: 15.10.1945. 444 numbered copies: 1–22 on hand-made Auvergne paper, 23–125 on deckle-edged Ingres, 126–444 on wove paper. [D21

ULMANN, André. *L'Humanisme du XXe siècle*. Paris, Éditions à L'Enfant Poète (1946). (Les jeunes humanistes.)

Frontispiece: Reproduction of a drawing dated 31.3.38. [D22

PETRARCA. *Cinq sonnets de Pétrarque* avec une eau-forte de Picasso et les explications du traducteur. A la fontaine de Vaucluse, 1947.

Imprint: 110 numbered copies, 1–100 and A–J. The translator has inscribed the number and a different sentence in each copy. [D23

KOVAČIČ. *La Fosse commune,* par Ivan Kovatchitch. Poème précédé du *Tombeau de Goran Kovatchitch,* par Paul Eluard. Paris, La Bibliothèque Française, 1948.

Édition de luxe: 110 numbered copies on deckle-edged Arches with an etching by Picasso.   [D24

BOLLE, Louis. *La Faucille et la lavande.* Frontispice de Picasso. Paris, G.L.M.

Imprint: April 1949. 415 copies: 1–10 on deckle-edged Marais, 11–390 on esparto paper, also A–Z, which are not for the trade.   [D25

GODET, Robert J. *L'Age de soleil,* avec une gravure de Pablo Picasso. Aux dépens de l'auteur. Paris 1950.

Imprint: 21.7.1950. Four private voucher copies, Nos. A–J on deckle-edged Arches with prints of five 'states' of the etching. Nos. I–C on deckle-edged Marais with the etching printed in black. Nos. 1–1000 with a reproduction of the etching.

The 'states' of the etching in the *de luxe* edition are in fact impressions of the same state in grey, terracotta and turquoise, as well as an impression from the copper plate in relief, which shows the black parts of the etching in white and the white parts in black. The Matarasso catalogue lists a second etching: a greatly stylized representation of a woman, dated on the plate: jeudi, 29 avril, 1944. Dr. Bernhard Geiser has given me the following information about this print: 'Picasso's gravure dated "jeudi 29 avril 1944" and called "La Torera" was added by

Robert J. Godet after the book had been completed. The title-page and the *justification du tirage* refer only to one gravure (portrait de l'auteur). The following notice was printed subsequently below the *justification:* "La gravure de Pablo Picasso 'La Torera' figurant dans les exemplaires de luxe a été tirée à cent seize exemplaires sur les presses de R. Lacourière, Maître tailledoucier à Paris".'

The copy which I inspected, in the collection of Colonel Daniel Sickles, Paris, did not contain this additional passage.   [D26

MOURLOT, Fernand. *Picasso lithographe.* 1950 and 1956. See E7, E8 and E13 below.

PENROSE, Valentine. *Don des féminines.* Préface de Paul Eluard. (Paris,) Librairie 'Les Pas Perdus'.

Imprint: 10.10.1951. Printed in 400 numbered copies and a few additional copies not for the trade, marked H.C.

Only the *édition de luxe,* Nos. 1–50, contains an etching by Picasso.   [D27

ROY, Claude. *La Guerre et la Paix.* Paris, Éditions du Cercle d'Art, 1954.

Édition de luxe: 100 numbered copies on deckle-edged Arches with a frontispiece lithograph signed by Picasso.   [D28

ARTAUD, A. *Autre chose que de l'enfant beau.* Paris, Broder 1957.

Imprint: 120 numbered copies on Japanese paper. The frontispiece, a coloured landscape etching by Picasso (see frontispiece), has no relation to the contents of the book. [D29

COCTEAU, Jean. *Témoignage.* [No place.] Pierre Bertrand.

Imprint: Oct. 1956. 125 copies on handmade Arches paper, signed by the author, with an etched frontispiece (nude) by Picasso, dated *Cannes, le 22.12.56.* There is another etching, by Lemagny, inserted in the book. Published on the occasion of Picasso's 75th birthday. [D30

PEPRATX-SAISSET, Henry. *La Sardane.* La danse des Catalans, son symbole, sa magie, ses énigmes. Lettre liminaire de Pablo Casals. Perpignan, Labau.

Dated at the end of the book: 1956. With a frontispiece (pen drawing reproduced by line block), which is repeated in green on the wrapper. The

drawing represents a group of dancers, above them a flying dove. [D31

SCHELER, Lucien. *Sillage intangible.* [Paris.] Le Degré Quarante et Un.

Imprint: 1958. 50 copies on Japanese paper. Contains an etching by Picasso, not related to the text. [D32

LEVEL, André. *Souvenirs d'un collectionneur* avec en frontispice une lithographie originale de Picasso et la reproduction d'une page autographe de Guillaume Apollinaire et de Max Jacob. Paris, Alain C. Mazo, 1959.

Imprint: 2200 numbered copies, 1–100 on handmade Arches with two prints of the lithograph ('en double état'), 101–2100 on Lourmarin paper, I–C as voucher and review copies. The frontispiece lithograph is not related to the text. [D33

E. BOOKS WITH A WRAPPER DESIGN

EXPOSITION de dessins et aquarelles de Picasso. Chez Paul Rosenberg du 20 octobre au 15 novembre 1919. Paris.

Wrapper design in auto-lithography. [E1

STRAWINSKY, Igor. *Ragtime pour onze instruments.* Transcriptions pour piano par l'auteur. Couverture de Pablo Picasso. Paris, Éditions de la Sirène, 1919.

1000 numbered copies, of which 1–100 printed in negative. In addition 10 voucher copies marked A–J. [E2

GEORGES-MICHEL, Georges. *Les Monparnos.* Roman nouveau de la Bohème Cosmopolite. Paris, Arthème Fayard et Cie.

Dated at the end of the text: 9.12.1923. Wrapper design in two colours after a gouache by Picasso. [E3

MINOTAURE. Revue artistique et littéraire. First Year, first issue. 1933.

Wrapper design in colour with the title of the review. [E4

EXPOSITION internationale, Paris 1937 Classe II. Groupe I. Conférence de Paul Eluard. Avenir de la poésie. A la Comédie des Champs-Elysées, le samedi 2 octobre à 16 h 15.

On the wrapper, Picasso's marginal drawing to *Grand air* by Eluard (*Les Yeux fertiles* 1936), greatly enlarged; the text of the poem is omitted and replaced by the words 'Avenir de la poésie'. [E5

BETTENCOURT, Pierre. *La Vie est sans pitié*. Saint-Maurice d'Etelan (1948).

Imprint: 101 numbered copies on wove deckle-edged Arches.

On the wrapper a reproduction of an etching from a line block. [E6

MOURLOT, Fernand. *Picasso lithographe*. Préface de Jaime Sabartés. Catalogue I. 1919–47. Monte Carlo, André Sauret.

Imprint: 25.10.1949. The wrapper (front and back) is lithographed, and the book also contains a lithograph as frontispiece. [E7

MOURLOT, Fernand. *Picasso lithographe*. Notices et catalogue, II, 1947–49. Monte Carlo, André Sauret.

Imprint: 25.11.1950. The wrapper (front and back) is lithographed, and the book also contains a lithograph as frontispiece. [E8

HOMMAGE à Henri Michaux.

Imprint: February 1951. 100 numbered copies. Programme in form of a double leaf, on the title-page a drawing reproduced by line block. [E9

SATIE, Erik. *Mémoires d'un amnésique*. Liège, Éditions Dynamo, Pierre Aelberts, éditeur. (Brimborions, 28.)

Imprint: September 1953. *Édition de luxe*: 40 copies on vellum paper, 10 on grey Dutch deckle-edged paper, one on Imperial Japanese paper, numbered 1–51. On the wrapper a drawing by Picasso reproduced in blue by line block, the title, in calligraphy, runs across the drawing. [E10

APOLLINAIRE, Guillaume. *Airelles*. Liège, Éditions Dynamo, P. Aelberts, éditeur, 1954. (Brimborions, 30.)

Imprint: 5.10.1954. *Édition de luxe*: 40 copies on vellum paper, 10 copies on rag paper, one copy on Imperial Japanese paper. The drawing on the wrapper is a portrait of the author by Picasso; the book contains further portraits of the author by Mambour, Marcoussis and Matisse. [E11

VERDET, André. *Provence noire*. Textes d'André Verdet. Photographies de Gilles Ehrmann. Couverture originale de Picasso. Paris, Édition Cercle d'Art, 1955.

Picasso's wrapper design consists of the words *Provence noire* and a slight sketch of a landscape. The drawing is dated 4.9.55. [E12

MOURLOT, Fernand. *Picasso lithographe*. Notices et catalogue, III, 1949–56. Monte Carlo, André Sauret.

Imprint: 6.X.1956. The wrapper (front, spine and back) is in lithography, and the book contains also a four-colour lithograph as frontispiece. [E13

PICASSO. *Dessins d'un demi-siècle*. Bergruen & Cie, 70, rue de l'Université, Paris-VII.

Imprint: 1956. On the reverse of the title-page: 'La couverture est une lithographie originale en quatre couleurs de Picasso, spécialement composée par l'artiste pour cette plaquette.' [E14

BOSQUET, Alain, and Pierre Seghers. *Les poèmes de l'année*. Couverture de

Picasso. Pierre Albert-Birot, Aragon (etc.). Paris, Seghers, 1956.

On the wrapper a recumbent Minotaur with a wine glass in the raised hand. [E15

GUTMANN, Dr. René-A. *Le diagnostic du cancer d'estomac à la période utile* (etc.). Paris, Doin & Cie, 1956.

A reproduction of a drawing by Picasso is pasted on the wrapper. The drawing, dated 12.5.56, shows a Herculean male nude hurling a spear at a lemuroid figure. [E16

(JACOB, Max.) Cadou, René Guy. *Esthétique de Max Jacob*. Portrait par Picasso. Paris, Seghers, 1956.

A selection from the letters of Max Jacob. On the wrapper a very naturalistic portrait drawing dating from 1915. *Édition de luxe*: 10 copies, A–J, on handmade Dutch Pannekoek paper. [E17

PEPRATX-SAISSET, Henry. *La Sardane*. 1956. See D31 above.

PICASSO [Pablo]. *Les Ménines 1957*. [Paris] Galerie Louise Leiris, 22 mai–

27 juin 1959. (Catalogue no. 10, Série A.)

Catalogue of an exhibition of Picasso's paintings. On the cover a lithograph in 4 colours. (See reproduction facing p. 94.) [E18

CLERGUE, Lucien. *Poesie der Photographie*, mit einem Vorwort von Jean Cocteau und einer Einführung von Jean-Marie Magnan. Verlag M. DuMont Schauberg, Köln. (1960.)

With a coloured title-page designed by Picasso and a coloured drawing by him on the wrapper, both dated 29.1.59. The title-page consists of six words in calligraphy (author, title, publisher) and the drawing of a photographer with camera. The drawing on the wrapper, a woman's head and a cock, has no connection with the text. [E19

GOLOMŠTOK, I.; SINJAVSKIJ, A. *Pikasso*. Moscow, Znanie 1960 [published 1961].

On the upper part of the wrapper a drawing (face with dove). [E20

F. MISCELLANEOUS

[PICASSO. *Poèmes et lithographies*. Paris, Galerie Leiris, 1954.] 50 numbered copies on deckle-edged Arches, further one copy each for the artist and for the printer. 14 lithographs in size 50 × 65 cm., each divided into 4 pages: 30 pages of drawings, 26 pages of text by Picasso in his own handwriting. [F1

ELUARD, Paul. *Un Poème dans chaque*

livre. Louis Broder. 'Ecrits et gravures.' Imprint: Paris 1956. 120 copies (1–100 and I–XX) on wove deckle-edged paper, the imprint signed by twelve artists who contributed to the book, among them Picasso. The book contains 17 prints (etchings and lithographs) by 15 different artists, including one lithograph by Picasso. [F2

Index of Authors

Numbers preceded by capital letters refer to the items of the Bibliography on pages 114–131.

Index of Authors